MONOGRAPHS OF THE
SOCIETY FOR RESEARCH IN
CHILD DEVELOPMENT

Serial No. 262, Vol. 65, No. 3, 2000

BREAKING THE LANGUAGE BARRIER: AN EMERGENTIST COALITION MODEL FOR THE ORIGINS OF WORD LEARNING

George J. Hollich
Kathy Hirsh-Pasek
Roberta Michnick Golinkoff

IN COLLABORATION WITH
Rebecca J. Brand
Ellie Brown
He Len Chung
Elizabeth Hennon
Camille Rocroi

WITH COMMENTARY BY
Lois Bloom

ii

MONOGRAPHS OF THE SOCIETY FOR RESEARCH IN CHILD DEVELOPMENT
Serial No. 262, Vol. 65, No. 3, 2000

CONTENTS

ABSTRACT

HOLLICH, GEORGE J.; HIRSH-PASEK, KATHY; and GOLINKOFF, ROBERTA
MICHNICK; in collaboration with BRAND, REBECCA J.; BROWN, ELLIE;
CHUNG, HE LEN; HENNON, ELIZABETH; and ROCROI, CAMILLE.
Breaking the Language Barrier: An Emergentist Coalition Model of
the Origins of Word Learning. *Monographs of the Society for Research in
Child Development*, 2000, **65**(3, Serial No. 262).

How do children learn their first words? The field of language development has been polarized by responses to this question. Explanations range from constraints/principles accounts that emphasize the
importance of cognitive heuristics in language acquisition, to social-
pragmatic accounts that highlight the role of parent-child interaction,
to associationistic accounts that highlight the role of "dumb attentional
mechanisms" in word learning. In this *Monograph*, an alternative to
these accounts is presented: the emergentist coalition theory. A hybrid
view of word learning, this theory characterizes lexical acquisition
as the emergent product of multiple factors, including cognitive constraints, social-pragmatic factors, and global attentional mechanisms.
The model makes three assumptions: (a) that children cull from multiple inputs available for word learning at any given time, (b) that these
inputs are differentially weighted over development, and (c) that children develop emergent principles of word learning, which guide subsequent word acquisition. With few exceptions, competing accounts of
the word learning process have examined children who are already veteran word learners. By focusing on the very beginnings of word learning
at around 12 months of age, however, it is possible to see how social
and cognitive factors are coordinated in the process of vocabulary development. After presenting a new method for investigating word learning,
the development of reference is used as a test case of the theory. In 12
experiments, with children ranging in age from 12 to 25 months of age,
data are described that support the emergentist coalition model. This

fundamentally developmental theory posits that children construct principles of word learning. As children's word learning principles emerge and develop, the character of word learning changes over the course of the 2nd year of life.

I. WHAT DOES IT TAKE TO LEARN A WORD?

Before children can tie their shoes, they have mastered thousands of words. At the outset (around 12 months of age), the character of word learning is slow and laborious with infants producing, on average, only two words per week (Carey, 1978). By approximately 19 months of age, however, children's vocabulary rapidly expands as they transform into what Pinker (1994) referred to as "vacuum cleaners" for words, acquiring up to nine new words per day (Bloom, 1973; Clark, 1973; Nelson, 1973; Templin, 1957).

The challenge for developmental psychology is to understand how children break the language barrier with their first words and turn into master word learners within a year's time. There have been a number of responses to this challenge. The constraints/principles theories emphasize the importance of cognitive heuristics in word acquisition (e.g., Markman, 1989; Merriman & Bowman, 1989; Waxman & Kosowski, 1990). Children operate with a set of word learning biases that assist them in linking words to objects, actions, and events. The social-pragmatic view, in stark contrast, highlights the role of parent-child interaction in priming word learning. Parents attuned to the child's intent supply the word for the relevant object, action, or event, thereby facilitating the child's lexical development (Nelson, 1988). Furthermore, the social-pragmatists assert that children are fundamentally social creatures and do not come to the word learning task "blind" to the essentials of communication (Carpenter, Nagell, & Tomasello, 1998). Rather, the children's driving need to communicate is the force that propels them to understand the meaning of a novel word (Bloom, 1993). Finally, the newest response to the word learning challenge is an associationistic account that highlights the role of "dumb attentional mechanisms" and memory processes. Children attach labels to the items that recruit their attention and stand out from the context. Calculating the frequency of co-occurrence between words and referents, children form the associations that constitute vocabulary acquisition (Plunkett, 1997; Smith, 1995, in press; Smith, Jones, & Landau, 1996).

1

While each of these potential answers to the word learning challenge seems plausible, we believe they are flawed in two ways. First, each emphasizes a single mechanism that is responsible for lexical development. Second, despite the fact that the character of word learning changes over the 2nd year of life (e.g., Clark, 1993; Golinkoff, Mervis, & Hirsh-Pasek, 1994), data in support of these theories are often from children who have already amassed a large number of words. Mechanisms used by expert word learners might not be characteristic of those used by novice learners.

To address these issues, in chapter 2, using these theories as a base, a new theory of word learning is presented, the emergentist coalition theory. The emergentist coalition theory offers a developmental account that explains the shift in word learning from the 1-year-old to 2-year-old as a change in the weighting of multiple factors, including attentional, social, and linguistic factors. In subsequent chapters, we offer a new method for testing this theory (chapter 3), data that substantiate the theory for the development of the "principle of reference" (Golinkoff et al., 1994) (chapters 4–6), and a discussion of how this theory can further a more complete understanding of word learning by embracing a hybrid view of this complex process (chapter 7). The remainder of this chapter contains an overview of the various approaches and the polarizing effect they have had on the field.

THEORIES OF WORD LEARNING

Current theories of word learning have been polarized by emphasizing a single word learning strategy to the relative exclusion of others (Golinkoff, Hirsh-Pasek, & Hollich, 1999; Hirsh-Pasek, Golinkoff, & Hollich, in press; Hollich, Hirsh-Pasek, Tucker, & Golinkoff, 2000; Woodward & Markman, 1998). Much of this polarization occurred in response to a philosophical conundrum introduced by Willard Quine (1960). This now all-too-familiar example involves a linguist, a foreign land, and a rabbit scurrying by. As the story goes, the linguist observes a native pointing to the rabbit and saying "gavagai" at exactly the moment the rabbit runs by. What is the linguist to think that *gavagai* refers to? Does it refer to the rabbit as a whole or to the rabbit's ears or to the rabbit's hopping, or even to the marks that the rabbit leaves in the soil? According to Quine, the world offers an infinite number of possible word-to-world mappings. Theories of word learning can largely be defined by whether they embrace this Quinean conundrum as a foundational assumption or whether they reject it. Theories that posit constraints or principles adopt Quine's view of the problem space. Theories that emphasize social input or associative learning consider Quine's example largely irrelevant to the problem of word learning. Each of these families of theories has staked out an important place in the literature.

The Constraints or Principles Theories

If Quine is to be taken seriously, the problem of word-to-world mapping is underdetermined, and the human mind must be equipped with constraints or principles that narrow the search space. Thus, this family of theories posits that the child approaches word learning biased to make certain assumptions over others for what a word might mean. Constraint theories have been posited for a number of cognitive development domains. For example, in discussing children's burgeoning knowledge of number, Gelman and Greeno (1989) wrote,

> If we grant learners some domain-specific principles, we provide them with a way to define the range of relevant inputs, the ones that support learning about that domain. Because principles embody constraints on the kinds of input that can be processed as data that are relevant to that domain, they therefore can direct attention to those aspects of the environment that need to be selected and attended to. (p. 130)

Similar statements have appeared in the literature on spatial development (Gelman & Greeno, 1989; Newcombe & Huttenlocher, in press) and object perception (Spelke, 1990). The general thrust of the constraints or principles position is to make a daunting task manageable by restricting the number of hypotheses the learner need entertain to arrive at a representation of a domain.

Clark (1983) and Markman (1987) first introduced the idea of word learning principles or constraints into the literature. Under Markman's whole object principle, for example, children assume that a word labels a whole object rather than an object part or attribute. Consistent with the Quinean thesis, if children made random word-to-world mappings, they could easily attach a name to the object part, to the object substance, or to the action in which the object is engaged. Positing a constraint like "whole object" necessarily reduces the ambiguity for the child and might explain how children learn words so rapidly in the 2nd year of life. Results from several studies support this principle. Among them, Markman and Wachtel (1988) presented 3-year-old children with novel names for objects that had a salient part. The experimenter then labeled the object and later tested whether the children attached the label to the salient part or to the whole object. If the whole object did not already have a name, children consistently labeled the whole object rather than the part.

3

If, in contrast, the whole object had a name that children knew, these children were more likely to assign the label to the object part. The whole object principle also holds that children will label objects over an interesting "nonobject" substance. For example, Woodward (1992) found that 18-month-old girls prefer to look at a moving nonobject display (e.g., a lava flow) over an unfamiliar boring object (e.g., a Chinese dumpling press) until a label is used. When the label is introduced, infants seemed to assume that this label referred to the object, and they attended relatively more to the boring object than to the interesting substance.

The whole object assumption is one of many constraints posited for early word learning. Over the last 15 years, there has been a proliferation of principles, including Waxman and Kosowski's (1990) "noun-category bias," Markman's (1989) "mutual exclusivity" (see also Merriman & Bowman, 1989), Markman and Hutchinson's (1984) "taxonomic assumption," and Clark's (1983) pragmatic constraint of "contrast." It was in the face of this growing number of proposed constraints that Golinkoff et al. (1994) posited a set of six principles, some new and some existing in the literature. The authors distilled the principles that were deemed necessary and sufficient to account for how children get word learning "off the ground." The Golinkoff et al. (1994) framework offered a developmental model in which the principles of word learning were organized on two tiers that captured the changing character of word learning. Fundamental to this framework was the idea that the principles themselves undergo change with development and are an emergent product of the combination of word learning experience and some inborn biases. The three lexical principles on the first tier were reference, extendibility, and object scope. The principles on the second tier were conventionality, novel name-nameless category (N3C), and categorical scope (see Figure 1).

Reference. Tier 1 represents the principles that are foundational to word learning; word learning could never begin without them. For example, it is hard to imagine word learning without the central principle of reference. It states that words symbolize, or stand for, objects, actions, or events. Furthermore, words have a status different from other sounds that are associated with objects such as the beep of the microwave or the ring of the telephone. These sounds occur at the same time that the object is present and embody a "goes with," or what Deacon (1997) called an indexical relation. Words function differently from sounds in that they have a "stands for" relation to what they label. Words do not need to occur contemporaneously or spatially coterminous with the objects, actions, and events they represent. Rather, words stand for their referents, even in contexts far removed from original usage or when the referents are not present. For example, mothers speak about "Daddy" even when Daddy is not home.

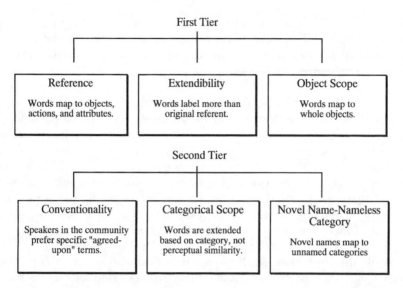

FIGURE 1.—The developmental lexical principles framework. The principles reduce the amount of information that children must consider for what a new word might mean; the first tier helps word learning begin; the development of the second tier coincides with the vocabulary spurt. (*Note.*—From "Early object labels: The case for a developmental lexical principles framework," by R. M. Golinkoff, C. Mervis, and K. Hirsh-Pasek, 1994, *Journal of Child Language, 21*, pp. 125–155. Copyright 1994 by Cambridge University Press. Adapted with permission.)

The development of reference is a mystery, a mystery that forms the cornerstone of this *Monograph.* Some have hypothesized that reference might emerge from prelinguistic communicative exchanges (Carpenter et al., 1998; Golinkoff et al., 1994). That is, linguistic reference might be the natural extension of the child's ability to comprehend and then produce points and eye gaze directed toward objects for the benefit of another. It is not clear, however, how pre-linguistic social exchanges become referential—even at a nonverbal level—or how linguistic symbols become "grafted" onto the nonverbal communicative process. Such a view displaces the problem of reference to an earlier time. Alternatively, Macnamara (1982) took reference to be a "primitive," available innately. This argument reduces to saying that no amount of data could get one to construct a concept like reference if it was not available from the start. In this sense, reference is akin to concepts like space and time, which philosophers like Kant have long argued are features of the human mind. Our view, however, is that reference develops from an immature to a mature state. By the time infants are learning their first words, the principle of reference is already available. Even 12-month-olds, at some level, assume that words refer. This principle, however, is not fully formed. As will be discussed in chapter 4, the mature development of reference can be traced to the second year of life, the product of the changing weighting of multiple cues.

Extendibility. This principle states that words do not refer to a single exemplar as do proper names, but to categories of objects. It could be otherwise. Each word could label only the original exemplar, as is the case when we call our own dog "Fido." Children in possession of the principle of extendibility, however, are not yet sure of what kinds of categories words label. As Clark (1983) documented, sometimes children extend their words based on color, sometimes on smell, and sometimes on shape. They will not be certain that words extend to objects in the same taxonomic category until the second tier, when the principle of categorical scope first appears (Markman & Hutchinson, 1984).

With the exception of children's very first words, which are sometimes used as proper names, the principle of extendibility seems to be present early in the 2nd year of life. Diary studies support the idea that children tend to extend their newly learned labels to other related objects (Barrett, 1978; Bloom, 1973; Dromi, 1987; Huttenlocher & Smiley, 1987; Mervis, Mervis, Johnson, & Bertrand, 1992). For example, Dromi (1987) found that a full 45% of Keren's first words were already extended to like objects. Huttenlocher and Smiley (1987) found that 1- and 2-year-olds' object names were readily extended to items within the same basic-level category.

A number of experimental studies that support the principle of extendibility have concentrated on the extension of labels to objects of similar shape. Smith, Jones, and Landau (1992) found that shape-based extensions were far more likely than those based on size, color, or material kind, particularly as children's vocabulary increased. By way of example, they found that 24-month-old children were most likely to accept a larger novel object that was the same shape and color as an original object as another "toma." An object that was a different shape, but the same size and color as the original object, was less likely to be called a "toma." Baldwin (1989) conducted a similar set of studies. She found that children (aged 2 years) would extend a novel word based on shape if asked to "find the dax" (where "dax" was the label previously given to an exemplar). Children did not extend based on similar shape, however, if they were simply asked to "find another one." Thus, shape-based extension, at least for 24-month-old children, seems to be specific to language labels. Though the experimental evidence for extendibility is obtained from children who are usually around 2 years of age, the diary data suggest that by the end of the 1st year of life, children have already reached at least a primitive realization that words label more than just the original exemplar.

Object scope. Words are mapped to children's representations of objects using the principle called "object scope." Object scope has two parts: Words refer to objects over actions or events, and words refer to whole objects as opposed to referring to an object part or an object's attributes. This principle is similar to Markman and Wachtel's (1988) whole object assumption reviewed above. In addition to the research noted for whole objects over parts or substances, there is now a growing literature supporting the claim that young children label an object over an action in which it participates.

By way of example, Echols (1991) used a video habituation procedure with 13- to 15-month-old children. The infants were shown novel objects performing novel motions. In one condition, infants saw multiple objects doing the same motion. In a second condition, the same object was presented undergoing different motions. Half of the infants in each condition heard a novel name as they watched the displays. Half did not. If the principle of object scope is operative then the novel label should heighten attention to the object over the action. Infants who heard labels should show more recovery when shown a novel object than when shown a novel action. If, in contrast, the label did not draw attention to the object, but rather to consistency in the video display, then children should dishabituate both to a novel action and to a novel object. The results offer compelling support for the principle of object scope. Infants who heard the novel label attended more to novel objects while those who heard no label attended to consistency in the video display.

These first three principles—reference, extendibility, and object scope—are sufficient to get the infant's word learning started. None of these require a great deal of linguistic sophistication, and they may be rooted in cognitive-perceptual development. Yet, they are essential to the word learning process. Nonetheless, they only allow the young child to learn words in a laborious, one-at-a-time fashion, not approaching the rapid word learning that occurs after the vocabulary spurt (Goldfield & Reznick, 1990). As the character of word learning changes around the time of the vocabulary spurt, these three principles alone cannot be the only mechanisms that account for the word learning process (for an alternative account see Elman et al., 1996). Reference, extendibility, and object scope, therefore, occupy what Golinkoff et al. (1994) referred to as the first tier in their word learning model. These first tier principles were constrained by the more sophisticated word learning principles which define the second tier. Thus, as a result of word learning experience, children form ever more refined hypotheses about the way words work.

Consistent with what Smith (in press) has argued, as children learn more words, their word learning strategies change. With experience, Smith claimed that children develop a "shape bias," noting that object names are extended based on shape. Next, we review the second tier principles.

Conventionality. The first tier principle of reference is constrained by the pragmatic principle of conventionality (Clark, 1983). While reference states that consistent phonological forms (words) map to entities in the environment (via the children's representations of those entities), the principle of conventionality makes it clear that for communication to proceed successfully, those consistent phonological forms should match the ones used by others in the environment. If young children are to be understood outside the family circle, they must abandon their invented, literally in-house words in favor of the more widely used terms.

Clark (1983) reviewed three kinds of evidence for conventionality. First, children use adult word forms. Second, they ask for the names of things from adults. Finally, they often spontaneously repair their own word choices. Moreover, children also tend to distinguish between home and public word choice. Thus, a child might call a pacifier a "pop" at home, but correctly refer to it as a pacifier when in public (Mervis, personal communication, as cited in Golinkoff et al., 1994).

Categorical scope. Extendibility is restricted by the second tier principle called "categorical scope," which refines extendibility by removing doubts about the basis for extension (see also Waxman & Kosowski's [1990] noun-category bias; Markman & Hutchinson's [1984] taxonomic assumption). The principle of categorical scope states that words label taxonomic categories, first at the basic level, and later, at the superordinate level (Golinkoff, Shuff-Bailey, Olguin, & Ruan, 1995). Thus, even though an orange and a basketball share many similar perceptual properties, including shape, children realize that they are not categorically linked. Perceptual similarity alone is no longer enough for extension; objects must be in the same taxonomic category.

In one study, for example, 3.5-year-old children initially categorized blackbirds with bats instead of with perceptually dissimilar flamingos. They quickly shifted, however, to putting blackbirds with flamingos when they found out that flamingos were called "birds," too (Gelman, 1987). In another study by Gelman, Croft, Fu, Clausner, and Gottfried (1998), 2- and 4-year-olds' extensions were not largely shape-based. Extensions, even for the youngest children, were often based on taxonomic kind. As the authors pointed out, this result occurred despite the fact that taxonomic kind was defined at the superordinate, as opposed to the easier, basic level. Finally, Shuff and Golinkoff (1998) reported that 2.5-year-olds (mean age 34 months) were willing to extend novel labels to items in the same taxonomic class as a target even when the taxonomic choice was highly dissimilar to the target. For example, when children were shown a high-heeled shoe (the target), a colored sneaker (the taxonomic choice), and a sliding board (the perceptual choice) drawn to look very much like the high-heeled shoe, they selected the sneaker when asked to "find another dax." In a no-word control condition, they did not select the taxonomic item above chance.

The ability to use a name to label a category of objects in the same taxonomic category, even in the absence of perceptually similarity, seems to be a process that evolves over time as children come to learn more about categories. Label extension is also sensitive to ontological category with perceptual similarity being more important for extension for categories of artifacts than for animal categories (Diesendruck, Gelman, & Lebowitz, 1998).

Novel name-nameless category. Finally, whereas the first tier principle of object scope allowed the child to map new terms to objects (as opposed to actions or object parts and attributes), the second tier principle of novel-name-nameless category helps the child to search out a nameless object referent as soon as a novel word is heard. N3C helps the child determine *which* whole object a new word should map onto. In a representative experiment, Golinkoff, Hirsh-Pasek, Bailey, and Wenger (1992) tested whether children, at 28 months of age, operate with the principle of N3C. Four objects were placed in front of the child—three of which were familiar (a ball, a shoe and keys) and one of which was unfamiliar (a tea strainer). The experimenter asked for the "glorp." Consistent with N3C, children selected the unnamed object as the referent for "glorp." In a control condition in which no label was used but children were just asked to retrieve an object, children gave the unnamed object at only chance level.

Markman's (1989) principle of mutual exclusivity (see also Merriman & Bowman, 1989) is similar to N3C, though N3C does not presuppose that children avoid having two names for things (Mervis & Bertrand, 1993; Mervis, Golinkoff, & Bertrand, 1994). N3C helps children engage in more rapid word learning because they search out an unnamed referent when they hear a novel name.

Constraints-based models: Conclusions. The two-tiered lexical principles model is a way of explaining how word learning begins and how it might change over development. Children begin word learning with the Tier 1 principles that enable them to attach a word to an object, action, or event. Tier 1 principles start out as domain-general in the Golinkoff et al. (1994) model and continually evolve into domain-specific principles as

9

word learning progresses. Tier 2 principles are the natural outgrowth of the painstaking word learning that goes on in Tier 1. Here, however, children have developed word learning heuristics that allow them to acquire vocabulary at a faster pace.

Thus, nested in the Golinkoff et al. (1994) framework was a powerful developmental solution to the Quinean dilemma. That solution rests within the head of the child. The child is predisposed to make certain hypotheses over others about word meaning thus reducing the problem of the indeterminacy of word-to-world mappings. It is only after these initial assumptions are made that the child, as constructivist, develops into an expert word learner.

The Social-Pragmatic Theories

In stark contrast to the constraints/principles view, social-pragmatic theories emphasize that children, embedded in a social nexus, are guided by expert word learners as they embark upon the word learning task (Carpenter et al., 1998). In this context, Quine's problem fizzles away because environmental input removes the ambiguity of the word learning situation. Nelson (1988) has written,

> The typical way children acquire words . . . is almost completely opposite of the Quinean paradigm. Children do not try and guess what it is that the adult intends to refer to; rather . . . it is the adult who guesses what the child is focused on and then supplies the appropriate word. (pp. 240–241)

Bloom (1993) similarly concluded that adults talk about objects, actions and events that children are already focused on, thereby producing language that is relevant to the child's interest. Children do not have to wade through alternative interpretations for a word; the correct interpretation is already the focus of their attention. Within the social context, children actively seek out information relevant to their interests and adults are happy to provide it.

Furthermore, there is considerable evidence that, by the end of the 2nd year of life, children are capable of utilizing social cues in the service of word learning (for a review, see Baldwin & Tomasello, 1998). In one representative study, Baldwin (1995) reported that 19-month-old children would not attach a label to an unnamed object if the speaker did not appear to be referring to the object. Children did not attach the label even if the object was interesting, even if the object appeared at the same time the label was uttered, and even if the speaker was touching the object (albeit in an apparently nonreferential manner). Thus, a child might hear an adult say, "There's a modi in here!" while the adult was looking into a bucket. Even if the adult first pulled out an object from a different bucket and only later pulled out the object from the original bucket, the child would nonetheless attach the label to the second, not the first, object they saw. Similarly, Tomasello and Barton (1994) had an experimenter pretend to look for a "toma." As each new toy was revealed, the experimenter scowled and put it back in its hiding place, as if to say, "This is not the toma." Only on the final toy would the experimenter look excited and hand the object to the child. Amazingly, 19-month-olds read the social cues and selected the correct toy as the "toma" on a later multiple-object comprehension test. Finally, Baldwin et al. (1996) showed that children could evaluate whether or not an adult uttering a label in great excitement ("It's a toma!") intended to label the object to which the child was attending or some other object. That is, 18-month-olds are not fooled into forming a link between a label uttered by a woman who is on the telephone just at the moment when those infants are focused on a novel toy. Thus, by approximately 18 or 19 months of age, children are sensitive to very subtle social cues when attaching a label to objects, actions, and events in the environment.

The case for children's social sensitivity to referential intent proves especially persuasive in the light of studies by Akhtar and Tomasello (1996). They found that 19-month-olds would attach a label to an object even if the labeled object were never subsequently revealed. Infants saw a series of objects hidden in various places around the playroom. The experimenter then went to one of the locations and said, "There's a modi in here," but pretended not to be able to get the object out of its hiding place. Next, in the training phase, all of the various objects were revealed, except the labeled object. Still, in the test phase, where duplicates of all the objects were available, infants selected the previously hidden object from amongst distractors. Further, Anselmi, Tomasello, and Acunzo (1986) found that 24-month-olds, when faced with an adult who apparently misunderstands what they are saying, would adjust their speech according to both that adult and the portion of the message they believe the adult misunderstood. Again, it is difficult to see how such behavior indicates anything other than a sophisticated understanding of the social function of language. This understanding could then be exploited in the service of word learning (but see Povinelli, Bering, & Giambrone, in press, for a dramatic example of how referential behavior, in chimps, does not necessarily indicate referential understanding; see also Povinelli & Eddy, 1996).

In sum, children in the social-pragmatic view are seen as skilled apprentices to expert word learners participating in a structured social world. Language comes as part of the package of being a human social animal. As Nelson (1996) argued, the language learning child faces the task any speaker and listener faces: ". . . to interpret the utterance of another within the context of the activity, as represented within the listener's current cognitive environment" (p. 137). If the child can "read" the social situation and if the adult is attuned to the child, then word learning becomes a kind of apprenticeship in which the social environment "feeds" word-to-world mappings to the child in digestible portions. A vast literature supports this claim. Children whose parents engage in joint attention such that those parents talk about what those children are looking at tend to have children with advanced vocabularies (Akhtar, Dunham, & Dunham, 1991; Masur, 1982; Tomasello & Farrar, 1986). In short, children are not plagued with too many options for word-to-world mappings. Rather, the cooperating adult limits the hypothesis space. On this view, then, Quine's linguist differs from real children in that children are immersed in rich social contexts that naturally delimit the possible mappings between words and their referents.

The constraints/principles and the social-pragmatic theories of word learning represent the most prevalent positions in the literature. A third position outlined by Smith (1995), Samuelson and Smith (1998), and Plunkett (1997) has recently been introduced to offer yet another perspective on the word learning problem. Collectively, their position could be called the associationist view of word learning.

The Associationistic View of Word Learning

Rejecting Quine's conundrum, authors like Smith (1995) and Plunkett (1997) suggested that word learning can be best accounted for through "dumb attentional mechanisms" like perceptual saliency, association, and frequency. It follows, therefore, that children do not need constraints or principles to forge word-to-world mappings. Rather, the process of mapping a word onto an object is straightforward. Children notice objects, actions, and events that are the most salient in their environment. They associate the most frequently used label with the most salient candidate. In this way, ambiguity in the word learning situation is removed. The most plausible word-to-world mapping surfaces as the only possibility. Thus, general cognitive mechanisms are sufficient to account for how young children first map words onto referents, and can combine in complex ways to account for the complexity of more sophisticated word learning.

To demonstrate how global cognitive mechanisms can more parsimoniously account for word learning findings, Samuelson and Smith (1998) replicated a study conducted by Akhtar, Carpenter, and Tomasello (1996). In the Akhtar et al. (1996) study, 20-month-old children played with three toys when their mother and two experimenters were in the room. A fourth toy was introduced when the mother and one of the experimenters left the room. Upon their return, they looked into a box containing the novel objects (including the fourth object) and said (of no object in particular) "I see a gazzer!" In a later object selection task in which the child saw all four objects, children consistently assumed that the toy introduced during the mother and experimenter's absence was the referent for the word "gazzer." Akhtar et al. (1996) ascribed children's performance to deep understanding of other persons' referential intentions. They concluded that children had apparently inferred that the object the adults had not seen during play must be the one being labeled "gazzer."

Samuelson and Smith (1998) disagreed with this explanation and created the same outcome—a word-referent mapping—by making the target object the most "novel-in-context" at the time the name was offered. They did this by moving the target object to a unique location (relative to the other objects) and putting it on a special blue tablecloth that glittered. They believed that their findings showed that the ambiguous linguistic event of figuring out which object the speaker is naming ". . . is resolved by mundane memorial and attentional processes" (p. 100). Although Samuelson and Smith (1998) did not deny the ultimate power of social knowledge, they believed that, for early word learning, their account was more compelling for its parsimony.

Further evidence in support of the domain-general approach comes from preliminary studies of connectionist modeling of word learning. Plunkett, Sinha, Moller, and Strandsby (1992) argued that there are no new systems that enter word learning at around the time of the vocabulary spurt. Instead, based on the functioning of their connectionist model, they argued that small and gradual changes in the underlying neural system could cause dramatic shifts like the vocabulary spurt. Indeed, their model mimicked this vocabulary explosion and even predicted that comprehension occurs in advance of production. It did this despite the fact that the only processes involved in the model were associative in nature. There were no a priori constraints or social skills built into this model. The data beginning to emerge from this theoretical perspective suggest that associative mechanisms play a crucial role in early vocabulary development.

CONCLUSIONS AND OVERVIEW OF *MONOGRAPH*

At this point, an interesting dilemma arises. The social-pragmatists predict, and find, that children are social beings, sensitive to very subtle cues to social reference. The associationists predict, and find, that children are distributional learners, sensitive to frequencies of multimodal mappings. Although there is mounting evidence in favor of the social-pragmatic and the associationistic accounts, however, the Quinean problem refuses to go away. Any single object, action, or event presents an array of possible referents to be named. By way of example, even something as simple as a "sippy cup" has a lid, an elevated portion on the lid designed for optimal sucking (the mouthpiece), a base, and possibly even some pink flowers on its blue plastic. Without some constraints on learning, how is the child to know which of these multiple parts is graced with the name, "cup"? All parts move together when the cup is lifted and some of these parts—such as the mouthpiece—may prove more salient than the whole object. The associationist would be left with the problem that the lid of the sippy cup is more salient than the entire cup. Indeed, until the child had much experience with many different kinds of cups labeled "cup" (some with no sippy part) the child could never solve the task at hand. That is, until the child has learned that words refer to whole objects that share shape (Smith, 1999, in press), the child might fail to attach a label to the whole object. The social-pragmatist is similarly doomed since every time a parent offers the cup, washes the cup, or drinks from the cup, all of the cup parts are equally available. Neither perceptually based nor socially based theories, in and of themselves, assist children in reaching the final destination that makes word-to-world mapping possible. Furthermore, once a name is bestowed, it could be extended along the lines of perceptual similarity (a plastic tent), function (a regular teacup), or taxonomic category membership (a squat red sippy cup with double handles). How is the child to know which aspect of the referent is being named and what governs extension? The answer lies in combining approaches. Just as the social-pragmatist and the associationist need the constraints/principles view, the constraints/principles theorists need the social-pragmatist and the associationist. Without social sophistication, how would children ever know to which of the many unnamed whole objects the speaker is referring? Without domain-general attentional mechanisms, how would the first tier principles develop?

From this discussion, three points become clear. First, multiple approaches are necessary. Without recognizing the enormity of the word learning problem a theory cannot support the weight of lexical acquisition. That is, like a table with only one leg, each theory makes a significant contribution but is insufficient to support and stabilize the table on its own. Just as a one-legged table is inherently unstable, scientific explanations of complex processes that force either/or decisions are not as powerful as those that embrace differing perspectives. What is required is a theory that culls from each of the major accounts of the word learning process. Second, the different accounts are often explaining the same phenomenon from different vantage points or different levels of analysis. That is, at one level, the associationists seem to focus principally on the domain-general "associative" mechanisms involved in word learning (and, indeed, all cognition). Conversely, the constraints/principles accounts focus on the language-specific, biased internal structures that develop (possibly as the result of domain-general mechanisms). At still another level, the social-pragmatists are primarily concerned with the socio-environment surrounding the child. Thus, with respect to referential understanding the associationist theory would build reference from the ground up, in an atomistic way, and the principle itself would be epiphenomenal. Children would behave *as if* they had a principle of reference when actually all they had was a set of associations between words and objects. At the next level of analysis, the constraints/principles view, reference is not just an epiphenomenon but an abstract principle that resides in the head of the child. The social-pragmatic theorist adopts an even more molar position, positioning the child in a social world. Children discover reference embedded in their everyday social interactions, guided by their social partners. (For a larger discussion of the idea that each of the different theories address a different level of implementation, see Hollich, 1999.) Finally, most of the studies that have been conducted in the literature on word learning, regardless of their theoretical orientation, generally are carried out with veteran word learners of 18 months or older. Yet, evidence for first-word learning must be collected from first-word learners. Methods must be developed that enable scientists to look at the word learning process from its earliest manifestation.

In this *Monograph*, we attempt to address these critical issues. In chapter 2, we present the emergentist coalition theory, a developmental account which combines aspects of the three prior theories. This model asserts that neither attentional, nor social, nor linguistic cues, in and of themselves, are sufficient for word learning. We next describe, in chapter 3, the overall design for the experiments presented in this *Monograph* and the new method we employ in the validation of this emergentist theory. Chapter 4 tests the predictions of the model with children at three ages (12, 19, and 24 months of age) using two novel objects, one much more attractive than the other. In this way, the attentional cue of perceptual salience is pitted against the social cue of eye gaze. Three such experiments are described that demonstrate the utility of the new method for studying the interaction of cues and the changes that occur in word learning, as well as illustrating the fragility of early word learning. Chapter 5 contains six experiments that focus on 12-month-olds' sensitivity to the increasing overlap of social cues. Although these studies reveal that 12-month-olds detected social signals, they did not seem to use these signals in the absence of multiple cues. Indeed, of the two experiments in this chapter that finally achieved word learning in 12-month-olds, one "bludgeoned" the children with 10 labels and many social cues, while the other showed that even five labels would work if the experimenter helped the children to spend more time looking at the target object as they heard the label. Chapter 6 addresses the question of whether early word learning is language-specific or whether any auditory stimulus can be associated with an object. Here again, multiple cues seem critical. While 12-month-olds were willing to link mouth noises to objects, they would not attach object noises to objects, unless the additional cue of salience was available. This suggests both that: (a) even very early word learning is to some extent domain-specific, and (b) only in the confluence of multiple cues can word learning take place. Finally, chapter 7 pulls the research together by revisiting our theoretical framework, the emergentist coalition model, in light of the research presented. The adoption of a developmental, multifaceted view of word learning is deemed essential to make progress on the difficult question of how word learning changes so dramatically in the 2nd year of life.

II. THE EMERGENTIST COALITION MODEL

Increasingly, researchers from the social-pragmatic, constraints/principles, and associationistic perspectives recognize the necessity of multiple factors from a number of domains in accounting for word learning. Indeed, Bloom and Lahey first embraced the true complexity of language and word learning in 1978, when they proposed the idea of mutual dependency between form, content and use. In 1993, Bloom wrote, "cognitive development bring the infant to the threshold of language only in conjunction with other developments in expression and social connectedness" (p. 52). Her continuing insistence (see Bloom, in press) on the child's role in actively coordinating multiple inputs to solve the word learning problem forms the foundation for the theory to be presented here.

Recently, other voices have joined the call for interactive theories. Baldwin and Tomasello (1998), for example, write the word learning "S requires an explanation encompassing both its social and cognitive roots" (p. 19). Finally, in a recent review of the field, Woodward and Markman (1998) explicitly state that none of the proposed solutions for the word learning problem is sufficient to explain how children acquire their first words. Rather, they write, "word learning depends on an ability to recruit and integrate information from a range of sources" (p. 371).

The emergentist coalition theory offers a hybrid approach that is sensitive to the multiple strategies children use to break the word barrier and to move from being novice to expert word learners. The complexity of word learning requires a model that embraces findings from the constraints/principles, associationist, and social-pragmatic literatures, thereby adopting a position that has been called "the radical middle" (Newcombe, 1998). The emergentist coalition model posits that children's lexical development is the product of intricate, epigenetic interactions between multiple factors. Principles in the constraints/principles theories are the *products* of attentional/associationistic factors in early development, which then become the *engines* of subsequent development. Likewise, the social-pragmatic expertise evidenced by 18- and 24-month-olds in word learning situations (e.g., Baldwin, 1995) is not present from the start. Rather, children must learn to exploit social interactions for their word learning potential. In brief, three main points come out of this "midline" position:

1. Children are sensitive to multiple cues, attentional, social, and linguistic, in word learning.

2. Children differentially weigh certain cues over others in the course of word learning.

3. Principles of word learning are emergent as each principle changes from an immature to a mature state.

This chapter outlines the theoretical basis for the emergentist coalition model providing a plausibility argument for each of these three assumptions. Subsequent chapters offer data to support the model.

CHILDREN ARE SENSITIVE TO MULTIPLE CUES IN WORD LEARNING

Attentional, social, and linguistic factors all play a necessary role in children's first word acquisition. As Markman (1992) has emphasized, "there tend to be multiple mechanisms for achieving the same endpoint" when a species faces an important problem (p. 90). We would emphasize, however, that although these mechanisms are available from the start, they might not be exploited to the same degree at different points in development. That is, whereas multiple cues may be available for word learning, the cues may not all be equally accessible to the young child. Several types of cues have been studied, including domain-general attentional factors, social information, and cues that emanate from the language itself.

Attentional Cues

Among the earliest influences on word learning are domain-general attentional factors such as perceptual salience, temporal contiguity, and novelty. As Deacon (1997) has emphasized, language is a relatively recent evolutionary addition. It could not long survive if it completely contradicted humans' attentional predilections. Humans are capable, for example, of detecting arbitrary relations in intermodal displays. This is certainly an advantage for "hooking up" referents and words. For example, Bahrick (1983) found that 9-month-old infants preferred to look at a display that portrays objects bouncing in temporal synchrony with an accompanying audio track, as opposed to a display that was not synchronous with the audio. Consistent with this finding, Gogate and Bahrick (1998) reported that 7-month-old infants learn the link between a vowel sound and an object when the movement of the object is synchronized with the production of the vowel sound. They do not learn this link when the object's movement is independent of the timing of the vowel sound or when the object does not move at all. This kind of associative correlation between sight and sound is what Deacon (1997) called an *indexical* link. Simultaneous attention to multimodal displays and the ability to find links between them is surely foundational to being able to learn the arbitrary relationships between words and their referents.

The novelty of an object also draws children's attention. In the presence of a word, children map a novel word to the novel object (e.g., Golinkoff et al., 1992). Aside from studies that manipulate referent novelty as part of addressing other word learning issues, there has been relatively little work on the effects of perceptual salience and temporal contiguity on word learning (but see Baldwin, 1991; Moore, Angelopoulos, & Bennett, 1999). This is probably due to the fact that word learning has been mostly studied in babies 18 months or older for whom the utility of such cues for word learning may be minimized.

Social Cues

Sensitivity to social cues during word learning has also been the subject of inquiry. Included among the social cues studied are sensitivity to eye gaze, pointing, and speaker intention. As Baldwin and her colleagues (e.g., see Baldwin et al., 1996) and Tomasello and his colleagues (see Carpenter et al., 1998, and Tomasello, 1995, for a review) repeatedly found, selective attention to information in the social environment is critical to word learning.

Eye gaze. The literature on early attention to eye gaze has produced stunning results. Scaife and Bruner (1975), for example, reported that infants as young as 8 months of age can follow the eye gaze of an adult (but see Corkum & Moore, 1995). More recently, Morales, Mundy, and Rojas (1998) found that even 6-month-olds begin to follow an adult's direction of gaze in experimentally controlled circumstances. Furthermore, 6-month-old attention to the direction of eye gaze correlates with receptive and expressive lexical development at 18 and 24 months. Research also indicated that by their 2nd year of life, infants recruit information from adults' eye gaze to assist them in learning new words, apparently reading the *intention* of the speaker in deciding the correct word-to-world mapping (Baldwin, 1991, 1993).

Pointing. The pointing literature is similarly rich. Between 12 and 14 months of age infants perform the conventional pointing gesture of extending an arm and the index finger toward some object, action, or event in their environment (Leung & Rheingold, 1981; Murphy & Messer, 1977; Schaffer, 1984). By 16 months of age, babies look at their social partner *before* they point, probably to make sure that their point will be perceived; at 10 months they check the adult's gaze *after* the point (Franco & Butterworth, 1996). By 17 months of age, infants start to realize the relationship between pointing and labeling. In fact, for 17- but not for 10-month-olds, looking time toward an object increased when a label accompanied pointing (Baldwin & Markman, 1989).

Social context. There is a vast literature on infants' sensitivity to social cues outside the word learning situation that is beyond the scope of this *Monograph* (e.g., Schaffer, 1984). The crux of this literature suggests that infants can attend to social information in their environment from a very early age. An ability to detect social information, however, is not the same as the ability to use social information in the service of word learning. Children may not realize the privileged status social cues have for word learning until they are well into their 2nd year of life. It may take time to recruit knowledge in one domain to serve another, as in other aspects of development. For example, in a classic study of meta-memory, Flavell, Friedrichs, and Hoyt (1970) reported that, whereas pre-school and kindergarten children could name the items on a list they were to memorize, it did not seem that they were using naming in service to memory. A similar finding in a different domain is from Hermer and Spelke (1996). Whereas young children can note the color of a wall in a room, they would not use that color as a landmark in a spatial task until much later. Harnessing and coordinating knowledge to serve varied ends is a hallmark of development.

Linguistic Cues

Along with the range of attentional and social cues available to children are cues from the language input itself, which help infants to find the words in the speech stream and identify their part of speech. Infants may eventually exploit these in making the correct word-to-world mappings. One of the first tasks the language learning child must face is determining the bounds of the linguistic system. That is, what kinds of sounds (or even gestures) fall into the category of language and are available for mapping to objects? Is the music made by the child's mobile language? Are the sounds that animals make language? Are various environmental noises, such as the beep of the microwave or the sounds of a truck, language? From birth, infants' brains seem to process linguistic stimuli differently than nonlinguistic stimuli (Molfese & Molfese, 1979).

This fact alone, however, does not ensure that babies can distinguish between words and other sounds for the purposes of forming mappings. Research by Balaban and Waxman (1997) suggests that by 9 months of age babies can tell the difference between a tone and a linguistic stimulus. By contrast, Woodward and Hoyne (1999) suggested that babies cannot distinguish between words and object noises for the purpose of forming mappings. Finally, Namy and Waxman's (1998) research suggests that at 17 months of age, gestures make just as good links with objects as do words! Clearly, more research is needed to understand when babies can tell the difference between words and other sounds.

Once they attend to speech, the second problem they face is that of *segmentation*, or finding the words in the stream of speech, served both by prosodic and distributional cues. Even before infants learn which words stand for which objects, actions, and events, they must first know where words begin and end. That is, infants must identify words within the speech stream. In spoken language, words are not separated by pauses as words in written language are separated by spaces. Yet by 7 months of age, infants are already able to remember words they have heard embedded in paragraphs (Jusczyk & Aslin, 1995). This means they must be conducting prosodic and distributional analyses in order to be finding words in the speech stream.

Prosody, or the melody of speech, includes the rhythm, stress, and intonation of a language. Infants appear to exploit a number of prosodic features to find the words (see Aslin, Jusczyk, & Pisoni, 1998; Jusczyk, 1997). As an example, infants at 9 months preferred to listen to words that have the stress pattern of their language (Jusczyk, Cutler, & Redanz, 1993). For English, this is a strong syllable followed by a weak syllable (as in "letter") as opposed to a weak syllable followed by a strong syllable (as in "guitar"). Thus, after 9 months of exposure to the native language—but not after 6 months—infants may be able to use this knowledge to reason that a strong syllable is the likely start of a new word. Although stress by itself cannot be infallibly used to find words, in combination with other prosodic cues (such as clause and phrase-final syllable lengthening, e.g., Bernstein-Ratner, 1986), it may help the infant solve the segmentation task. In addition, the exaggerated intonation and pitch of child-directed speech increases babies' attention to speech, in effect, telling them, "this talk is for you." Recent evidence suggests that infants identify familiar words and learn novel words better when delivered in child-directed rather than adult-directed speech (Fernald, McRoberts, & Herrera, in press; Golinkoff, Hirsh-Pasek, & Alioto, 1998).

Perception of, and memory for, syllabic sequences are also essential for finding the words—as is shown by work of Saffran, Aslin, and Newport (1996; see also Aslin, Saffran, and Newport, 1998). In their work, it appeared that 8-month-old babies were computing the transitional probabilities between syllables from only a brief exposure to a string of syllables. A monotone, repeating sequence of syllables (e.g., "bidagola...") was played to the babies for 2 min, after which they showed a greater preference for listening to new syllables that violated the transitional probabilities of the items in the set over equally frequent syllable sequences that did not violate these probabilities. Thus, the ability to break up the speech stream into wordlike units seems to be in place by the time children embark on their word learning journey. From exposure to a variety of distributional and prosodic cues, infants come to weight the characteristics of their native language more heavily than nonnative characteristics. Increasing sensitivity to these characteristics assists the child in the segmentation task so essential for word learning.

Finally, grammatical information found in morphology and syntax can affect how children make the link between words and the appropriate referent. In particular, the syntactic reflexes associated with the different parts of speech are available to help children figure out what a novel word is labeling. For example, Katz, Baker, and Macnamara (1974) and Gelman and Taylor (1984) reported that 17-month-olds were sensitive to the presence or absence of an article for deciding whether a novel word is a common or proper noun. Similarly, it appears that children can direct their attention to an object when asked to look at "the blick," and to an action when "blicking" is requested (Echols, 1998). Furthermore, children will focus specifically on the properties of the object when "a blick one" is requested (Hall, Waxman, & Hurwitz, 1993; Klibanoff & Waxman, 1999). More strikingly, in an experiment using cortical evoked potentials, Shafer, Shucard, Shucard, and Gerken (1998) showed that 10-month-olds gave different event-related potential responses to passages in which the article "the" had been replaced by a nonsense syllable than to normal passages. This suggests that by 10 months, babies have analyzed the phonological and prosodic properties of "the" and notice when it is replaced.

Subtle grammatical distinctions may well aid children in making the appropriate word-to-world mapping at least by about 18 months of age. Prior to that time, however, little is known about what infants know about these grammatical cues to part of speech. Waxman and Markow (1995) found that, at 12 months, babies seemed oblivious to the use of a noun or adjective construction in a manual habituation task. Additional research is needed to see how early infants can detect such morphological and syntactic cues and when they use them in the service of word learning.

Our first major hypothesis is that multiple cues (attentional, social, and linguistic) are available to the young word learner whenever language is heard. The question remains as to when the young child can access or recruit these cues in service to word learning.

CHILDREN DIFFERENTIALLY WEIGH CERTAIN CUES OVER OTHERS IN THE COURSE OF WORD LEARNING

The basis for the second hypothesis is that the young child cannot access all these cues from the start. Over developmental time, children differentially weight the different types (attentional, social, and linguistic) of available information for word learning. Thus, for example, in the principle of extendibility, perceptual similarity (Smith, Jones, & Landau, 1992) may initially be weighted heavily only to give way to extension on the basis of taxonomic membership, as defined by function (Kemler Nelson, 1995) and object kind (Gelman et al., 1998; Shuff & Golinkoff, 1998).

A similar story could be told about the development of the principle of reference—which comprises the remainder of this *Monograph*. It is possible that young children first map a word onto the most perceptually salient object in the environment, as if words are hooked to objects from their point of view and not the speaker's. This notion of perceptual salience is ambiguous in that it can be thought about in two distinct ways. First, salience can be treated as a task demand. In a behavioral sense, words are attached to that which attracts attention (Smith, in press). Alternatively, salience can be thought of as a *cue*, in that when children hear a new word, they assume that the word maps to the most salient object available. The former requires only a "dumb attentional mechanism" (Smith, in press); the latter requires that children have a hypothesis about what it is that adults are likely to label—the interesting object. Each of these perspectives on salience results in the same outcome, and they are treated as functionally equivalent in this *Monograph*. With development, infants may come to recognize that social cues, and not perceptual cues, are more reliable for mapping words to objects. They may eventually learn to map words onto objects, actions, and events from the speaker's point of view. Figure 2 depicts this shifting of weights as it might apply to the principle of reference.

The general thrust of this hypothesis is that not all inputs to word learning are created equal. The character of word learning changes in fundamental ways over time as children come to weigh some inputs more heavily than others. Woodward, Markman, and Fitzsimmons (1994) suggested such a possibility when they wrote that children might begin the word learning process by using "brute force" to associate labels with their referents. It is important to remember that from our theoretical perspective, however, children (at least by 12 months of age) are always operating with a principle of reference, although the cues they rely on will change over time.

If it is the case that young children emphasize certain cues over others in the word learning situation and if the weighting of these cues changes with development, it is incumbent upon researchers to: (a) track these

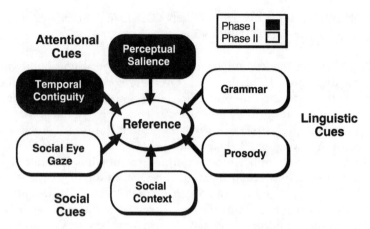

FIGURE 2.—The coalition model implemented for reference: Children shift from a reliance on attentional cues, like perceptual salience, to a greater dependency on social and linguistic cues, like eye gaze and grammar.

changes, and (b) describe the mechanisms that could account for them. A developmental theory must demonstrate not just *that* a change occurs, but *how* it occurs. Borrowing from the coalition model of grammatical development (Golinkoff & Hirsh-Pasek, 1995; Hirsh-Pasek & Golinkoff, 1996a), the emergentist coalition model for word learning suggests an important mechanism of change is what Hirsh-Pasek and Golinkoff called "guided distributional learning." Because learners are biased to note certain inputs over others (such as novelty, temporal contiguity, or prosody), word learning is "guided" from the outset. It is as if learners start the task of word learning with "heat seeking missiles" that guide them to just the right sort of language-relevant information in the environment. Such a hypothesis is common among developmental researchers, as biases of these sorts have been posited for numerous domains including number, object concept, and language (see Karmiloff-Smith, 1992, for a review).

In addition to being guided, however, as children receive language input, the nature of their learning also is shaped through attention to distributional information. Thus, even if children are born with a bias to note perceptually interesting objects in their environment, they will come to realize that the perceptually interesting object is not always that one that "gets the name." How might they discover this? When a mother is on the telephone, for example, she is likely to say any number of words while the child is playing with the exciting toy train. Potentially, the child could think that the train is called any number of things, from "hello" to "goodbye." None of these "labels," however, is ever consistently associated with the train when the mother is off the telephone. For that matter, only when the mother looks directly at the toy is any word consistently present. Thus, "train" is the most frequent, most consistent word provided for the toy, *and* more important, eye gaze is the strongest, most consistent cue to that reference. Across a number of examples, children may come to realize, pragmatically, that eye gaze is a good indicator of the consistent mapping, and they may come to follow it, or make use of it in directing attention. In essence, the mechanism of guided distributional learning asserts that children are sensitive to a wide range of cues and events in the world around them and, more important, that they are sensitive to the frequency of the co-occurrence of these cues. Ultimately, the consistent correlations, no matter how subtle, come to dominate (see Hollich, 1999, for a more detailed discussion of this mechanism).

Thus, in the emergentist coalition model of word learning, we build a baby who attends to eye gaze from the outset of word learning, but may not use eye gaze in the service of word learning. The child has to learn through experience which cues (such as eye gaze) are more likely to facilitate the process of word learning. Computing the reliability of cues in making consistent mapping provides the catalyst that shifts the balance from weighting perceptual salience more heavily to weighting social information more heavily. In this way the child comes to rely on social cues and uses the speaker's intent to inform word-to-referent connections. Put simply, children will hear more word-referent pairings for the correct choice, and will be wrong less of the time, if they attend to social cues.

Recent research shows that infants can detect simple correlations among cues to form categories (Saffran, Aslin, & Newport, 1996; Younger & Cohen, 1983, 1986; Younger & Fearing, 1998). In one representative study, infants who were 8 months of age detected the transitional probabilities in phonemes delivered in an artificial language. Infants formed categories of syllables that did and did not share the same transitional probabilities, preferring at test to listen to syllables that maintained these probabilities over ones that had different probabilities. Finally, a number of studies by Younger and her colleagues reported that infants in their 1st year of life could detect the co-occurrence or correlation of body parts of schematic animals to form categories. Younger and Fearing (1998), for example, reported that 12-month-olds could detect correlations among the body parts of animals and preferred examining a novel animal that violates the established pattern of correlation compared to a novel animal that maintained the same correlations.

Studies like these add plausibility to the hypothesis that young children should be able to detect cross-modal correlations in the word learning situation. Furthermore, recent neurological evidence can be seen to substantiate the behavioral findings. As Hebb (1949) long ago noted, neurons that fire together, wire together. Detection of correlations is one of the main learning mechanisms of neural networks (Bates & MacWhinney, 1987; Elman et al., 1996; Rolls & Treves, 1998). Thus, it is not surprising that correlation may be a primary learning mechanism in the acquisition of language.

In sum, we posit that children have certain learning biases and that these biases become the grist for the infant statisticians who are just learning how words work. These biases are not fixed in stone. They change and adapt to the word learning situation. For example, once children note that perceptual cues are not reliably correlated with word mapping, they will alter their strategy to make more use of social information, hence more heavily weighting this information relative to perceptual information.

PRINCIPLES OF WORD LEARNING ARE EMERGENT; CHILDREN MOVE FROM USING IMMATURE TO MATURE WORD LEARNING PRINCIPLES

Constraints or principles are emergent. Much like the pattern of waves on a beach, formed from a multitude of factors (such as wind, tide, bottom shape, and water density), children similarly respond to the interaction of multiple factors in the word learning situation. The behavior that results is more than the sum of each individual cue. Only through the combined action of all sources of information can the process of word learning proceed apace. Remove any cue, and word learning becomes much more difficult, if not impossible.

As the constraints or principles develop over time, they move from an immature to mature state. From the multiple cues surrounding them in word learning contexts, children gradually cull more sophisticated heuristics for word learning. They implicitly test their current theories, shift the weights of the cues, and subsequently alter their word learning principles. Early versions of the principles are refined in ways that make word learning faster and more precise (Golinkoff et al., 1994).

This shift from immature to mature principles may also embody a change from domain-general attentional factors to domain-specific language factors. The principle of object scope provides a working example. Early in development, children are biased to look at whole objects segmented from other objects by common fate (Kellman & Spelke, 1983; Spelke, 1994). This domain-general bias is seen across a range of phenomena and also proves very useful for children learning their first object words. There are words, however, for object parts, object properties, and actions. To be a full member of the word learning community, children will need to learn the domain-specific manner in which they can violate the whole object assumption. For example, Waxman and her colleagues (Hall, Waxman, & Hurwitz, 1993) found that 4-year-olds, but not 2-year-olds, can use grammatical cues in tandem with perceptual cues to note that a word maps onto an object property ("a fepish one" for the toy with the stars on it) or an action (e.g., "see fepping"). Thus, early domain-general preferences can be supplanted with more precise language-specific strategies to facilitate word learning.

The case for movement from an immature to a mature state also can be illustrated with respect to the principle of reference that will be highlighted in this *Monograph.* We hypothesize that children with an immature principle of reference might assume, in a domain-general manner, that words label the most perceptually salient object in the environment. In contrast, more mature learners might realize, through guided distributional learning, that social cues are better indicators of word-to-world mappings. This shift in emphasis reflects a very basic change in the child's working hypotheses about word learning. At first, children's strategies are dominated by their own point of view. Words label what the child has in mind. That is, reference is dominated by the child's tendency to associate a word with the object, action, or event that is temporally contiguous and/or perceptually salient, much as they learn the link between any two contiguous events. Later, as noted in the train example above, the child comes to perceive the intentionality of others and can then become an apprentice to a master language user. The child comes to realize the full symbolic nature of language. Baldwin (1993) wrote,

> Infants' ability to distinguish referential from non-referential acts has important implications for the course of language learning. . . . It enables them to correctly ignore coincidental word-object pairings that not infrequently occur in the rapid flux of human action and interaction. . . . Innumerable potential mapping errors may thus be avoided. (pp. 841–842)

The keys to this shift in word learning are: (a) the child's ability both to recognize relevant social cues and to realize that they can be recruited in the service of word learning, and (b) the ability to shift attention from the object that currently dominates the child's focus of attention to the object which is the adult's intended referent. Both of these factors have been investigated in the literature and provide the working hypotheses for the research to follow.

When do children realize that social cues are relevant to the word learning situation? We know from the research described above that infants are attuned to social information in their environment before they learn their first words. Research by Baldwin and her colleagues (Baldwin, 1993, 1995; Baldwin & Tomasello, 1998), however, suggests that it is not until 18 or 19 months of age that infants begin to recruit this knowledge in the service of word learning. Not only do infants younger than 18 months have trouble harnessing social cues for word learning, but, perhaps as a consequence of this limitation, they often fail to attach a label to an object that is not in their immediate focus of attention. Tomasello and Farrar (1986) first introduced the relevant literature on this topic in a now classic experiment. Two objects were labeled either in an "attention-following" procedure or an "attention-switching" procedure. In the attention-following case, adults labeled an object with which the child was currently engaged. In the attention-switching case, the experimenter waited until the child was not playing with either object and then drew her attention to the labeled object. Only in the attention-following case was infants' comprehension significantly above chance. Subsequent experiments by Dunham, Dunham, and Curwin (1993) revealed that this effect was not due to a lack of motivation on children's part or to a greater amount of attention spent on the labeled object in the attention-following condition (but see Flom, Phill, Pick, & Burch, 1999). Rather, even when attention was allocated equally to objects in both conditions, children were more likely to learn a label for objects in the attention-following condition. Thus, at an early age, children seem unable to use parental eye gaze to reliably assign word to referent. Adamson (1995) found that parents who name objects from their young infant's focus of attention—rather than from their own—produce toddlers with increased vocabulary relative to their peers (see also Carpenter et al., 1998; and Tomasello & Akhtar, 1995). It is only after 19 months of age that children can use the adult's focus of attention to assign a word-to-world mapping.

Taken together, these studies pinpoint a central difference between the immature and the mature principle of reference. Immature reference is dominated by the child's point of view. Unable to capitalize on the social cues provided by their mentors, children with an immature principle of reference are trapped in a limited word learning situation. They must wait for the moment when an adult repeatedly labels the object already in their focus of attention. In contrast, mature word learners can adopt the speaker's point of view and capitalize on the rich storehouse of knowledge that others bring to bear in the word learning situation. These children can shift their attention to the speaker's focus and can greatly expand the number of potential labels that can be learned in any given encounter. Word learning in this scenario can proceed at a rapid pace. Equipped with an immature principle, infants can get word learning off the ground. With the mature principle, they can fly.

This *Monograph* will focus on the principle of reference as a test case for the emergentist coalition model. This is not the first time that researchers have attempted to understand the development of reference and its relationship to word learning. Researchers such as Vygotsky (1962), Werner and Kaplan (1950), and Piaget (1926) were all concerned with the mechanisms underlying word learning. Piaget posited that at the close of the sensori-motor period, children constructed symbolic representations of a nonlinguistic nature that paved the way for word learning. Vygotsky (1962) argued that even children's initial words are communicative acts, first learned and used in social situations and only later becoming available as instruments for thought. According to Werner and Kaplan (1950), words start out as close associates to their referents. For example, words initially sound like what they represent (phonetic symbolism). Later, words are extended based on similarity in shape or color or size. Finally, words apply abstractly to concepts that need share no surface similarity. In more recent times, McShane (1979) argued that children experience a "naming insight" when they suddenly recognized that all objects have names, though the underlying process was left undefined. Thus, prior theorists speculated about the nature of reference. The emergentist coalition model offers a new look at an old question and a new way of viewing the relationship between the predominant theories of word learning.

SUMMARY

The emergentist coalition model is a hybrid model based on three assumptions: (a) that children are exposed to multiple inputs; (b) that the weighting of these inputs change over time through guided distributional learning; and (c) that the result of this process is emergent principles of word learning that move from immature to mature, from domain-general to domain-specific, principles. As children develop they not only construct more precise strategies for word learning but also come to recruit more of the available cues into the process.

Having staked out the theoretical basis for the emergentist coalition model, it is imperative to ask whether this model can be validated experimentally. Using the principle of reference as a test case, we hypothesize: (a) that children are attentive to both perceptual and social cues in a word learning task; (b) that perceptual cues are more heavily weighted for beginning word learners such that they will not be able to use social cues, such as eye gaze, to label a more boring over a more interesting object; and (c) that as infants learn to use social cues in word learning, they are better able to attach labels in attention-switching situations and to discover the intentionality of adults.

III. THE INTERACTIVE INTERMODAL PREFERENTIAL LOOKING PARADIGM

Camille Rocroi

The emergentist coalition model makes clear predictions about how words are learned. To evaluate these hypotheses, however, we needed to go beyond existing methodologies to develop a method that: (a) could be used with both infants and older children; (b) made minimal response demands on children; and crucially, (c) allowed for the manipulation of multiple cues from the attentional, social, and linguistic realm within one paradigm. Other methods used to study word learning satisfy some, but not all, of these requirements. For example, Werker, Cohen, Lloyd, Stager, and Cassosola (1998) used a version of the habituation paradigm called the "switch design" to study word learning in 14-month-olds. This method does not allow for the manipulation of social cues. The Intermodal Preferential Looking Paradigm (IPLP; described below) suffers from the same shortcoming (Hirsh-Pasek and Golinkoff, 1996b). Finally, Woodward et al. (1994), Tomasello and Akhtar (1995), and Baldwin (1993) used controlled naturalistic interaction followed by multiple choice tests. Although these tasks permit the manipulation of social cues, they require overt behavioral response to experimenter requests, something that younger infants cannot do. Thus, the Interactive Intermodal Preferential Looking Paradigm (Interactive IPLP) was developed to satisfy all the requirements described above (Hollich, Hirsh-Pasek, & Golinkoff, 1998).

The Interactive IPLP has its roots in work done by Baldwin (1991) and Fagan (1971; Fagan, Singer, Montie, & Shepard, 1986). Principally, however, the Interactive IPLP is a modification of the IPLP developed by Golinkoff, Hirsh-Pasek, Cauley, and Gordon (1987; Hirsh-Pasek & Golinkoff, 1993, 1996a, 1996b). In the standard IPLP (originally adapted from Spelke, 1979), the infant is seated on a blindfolded parent's lap in front of two laterally spaced video monitors. A concealed centrally placed audio speaker plays a linguistic stimulus that matches only one of the displays shown on the screens. The total amount of time (measured to hundredths of seconds) that the infant spends watching the matching versus the nonmatching screen is calculated both online by a hidden observer and through subsequent scoring from a video record. To see how this works, consider the case of noun comprehension (Golinkoff et al., 1987; Hirsh-Pasek & Golinkoff, 1996a, 1996b; Hollich, Hirsh-Pasek, & Golinkoff, 1998). A light between the two monitors directs the child's attention toward the center, and a linguistic message (produced in child-directed speech) is delivered from the centrally placed but concealed speaker. On one screen, the child sees a boat and on the other a shoe, and the linguistic message is, "Do you see the boat? Find the boat!"

The logic of this procedure, which has been consistently confirmed, is that children look more quickly and longer at the screen displaying the targeted object (the boat) than at the screen displaying the nontargeted object (the shoe). That is, infants give more attention to the video event that matches what they are hearing, in this case, the linguistic message, than to a video event that does not match. In no studies performed in our laboratories have children ever shown a significant preference for the nonmatching screen. This logic has ecological validity. Parents often comment on the actions, objects, and events surrounding the child, intending to direct the child's attention. A large portion of the adaptive advantage conferred by language depends on orienting in a manner consonant with the language message.

The major advantages of the standard paradigm are numerous. First, only a looking response is required from the child. Children do not have to point, answer questions, or act out commands. This permits testing at very young ages, even as young as 4.5 months of age (Spelke, 1979). Second, the video monitors can represent dynamic stimuli. This is critically important for the study of verbs, as well as for the study of complex syntactic constructions. Third, children are able to take advantage of a coalition of syntactic, semantic, and prosodic information all online. That is, just as language learning occurs amidst a coalition of cues that are rarely, if ever, separated in the actual input to the child, the IPLP can present these cues in concert as well.

For these reasons, the standard IPLP has proven very useful in the study of early language. Some of the results thus far have indicated that infants appear sensitive to cues for constituent structure by 14 months of age (Hirsh-Pasek & Golinkoff, 1996a), to the meaning of common nouns and verbs by 16 months of age (Golinkoff et al., 1987), to word order by 17 months of age (Hirsh-Pasek & Golinkoff, 1996a), to the verbal morpheme /ing/ by about 18 months of age (Golinkoff, Hirsh-Pasek, & Schweisguth, in press), and to the meaning implications of transitive and intransitive sentence frames by 24 months of age (Hirsh-Pasek & Golinkoff, 1991,

1993, 1996a; Naigles, 1990). In each case, the paradigm has been a sensitive measure of children's lexical and syntactic knowledge.

For the purposes of early word learning research, the standard paradigm provides an excellent foundation. For example, babies as young as 15 months of age (Schafer & Plunkett, 1998), presented with six repetitions of a word, were able to learn new words in this paradigm. Yet, it could be argued that the paradigm vitiates the need for social cues, because it artificially limits the range of choices for making a mapping. Recall that the stimuli are presented on video screens in the dark. Therefore, to study word learning in a way that more closely mimics what takes place in the real world, we must overcome the inability of the standard IPLP to permit social interaction. Many believe that these interactions between children and adults are critical for the word learning process, particularly at early ages (Adamson, 1995; Baldwin & Tomasello, 1998; Tomasello & Farrar, 1986). As a result, the standard procedure was expanded in ways that would permit the study of early word learning in the context of social interaction (Hollich, Hirsh-Pasek, & Golinkoff, 1998). The Interactive IPLP incorporates real, three-dimensional objects and a live experimenter. It was developed to increase ecological validity while at the same time maintaining strict experimental control.

OVERVIEW OF THE INTERACTIVE IPLP

The Interactive IPLP is depicted in Figure 3. A child is seated on his mother's lap across the table from the experimenter. After playing with two toys, the experimenter labels one of the toys (e.g., "This is a glorp"). In a subsequent test phase, the child sees the two toys presented side-by-side on a display board. The now hidden experimenter requests the target object. As in the standard paradigm, it is hypothesized that children who learn the label will look longer at the target object than at the non-target object.

Even this brief description of the paradigm reveals some of its strengths as a method for investigating early word learning. First, the procedure allows us to separately manipulate attentional, social, and language cues. By way of example, in some of the studies reported here, attentional cues like perceptual salience were varied. In these "unequal salience" studies, children were presented with an interesting and a boring object, whereas only the interesting (or boring) toy was labeled. In this manner, children's sensitivity to perceptual salience as a word learning cue was tested. If children assumed that a label maps onto the most perceptually salient object, then they should have attached the label to the interesting object even when the experimenter labeled the boring toy. Likewise, a host of

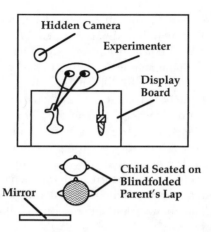

FIGURE 3.—Interactive IPLP: A hidden camera records children's looking preferences toward two objects on a display board. The mirror allows view of the experimenter's actions.

interactive social cues also can be manipulated in the interactive paradigm. For example, in some conditions, the experimenter labeled the target object by looking in the direction of that object. In other conditions, the experimenter touched, pointed to, or handled the object while delivering the label. Similarly, language cues can also be manipulated in the paradigm. In some of the experiments, words were compared to "mouth noises" and other nonlinguistic sounds to assess whether the processes involved in labeling were language-specific. In short, one major advantage of this paradigm is that multiple interactive cues can be manipulated within the word learning setting.

Second, an additional advantage is that it can be profitably used with children of multiple ages. Unlike habituation paradigms that are more suited to infants, and pointing and acting out tasks that are age appropriate for toddlers, the Interactive IPLP can be used for cross-sectional designs with infants and toddlers. Thus, children who are just breaking the word barrier can be compared with children who are undergoing or who have undergone the vocabulary spurt. These dual advantages of the interactive paradigm are more clearly revealed in a detailed examination of the specific procedure and design used in the studies presented in this *Monograph*.

Apparatus

The infants were seated on a blindfolded parent's lap 75 cm back from the center of the modified Fagan board that sits on a table. This

33

modified board consisted of a (55 cm × 50 cm) base, and a hinged (40 cm × 50 cm) board. The display board was painted black on one side with Velcro attachments at 20 cm from the top and 12.5 cm from either side (providing two sites for attaching objects 30 cm apart). The board was hinged such that it could rotate lengthwise, pivoting to hide or reveal whatever objects might be attached, and thereby providing precise control over the duration of exposure. Timing of the presentation was accomplished by use of a specially designed timer (Infant Test Timer), which could be set to produce a brief tone when the requisite period had elapsed. A mirror behind the infant allowed the video camera to record the reflection of the objects on the board and the behavior of the experimenter (except when she was hiding behind the board during salience and test phases). The infant's looking responses were captured on the video at the same time.

Procedure

Infants came into the language laboratory after parents were contacted via a commercially available birth list (Temple laboratory) or from birth announcements in the local paper (Delaware laboratory). While the infant settled into the playroom, the parent completed the MacArthur Communicative Developmental Inventory (CDI). The infant CDI was presented to parents of children who are 16 months of age and younger; the toddler form was administered to parents of older children up to 24 months of age (Fenson et al., 1994). The CDI provided an independent measure of the infant's comprehension and production. For reasons discussed in the general discussion of chapter 7, however, the CDI did not correlate well with our empirical tests. Detailed data from it are not reported here (except to parenthetically note the mean number of words in the productive vocabulary of the children we studied). When the infants were comfortable, they were seated on a parent's lap in front of the apparatus. The parent put on a visor or blacked out sunglasses to cover his or her eyes and testing began.

Design

The general design consisted of two sets of alternating familiar and novel trial blocks. Each familiar trial block was comprised of an exploration phase and a test phase (consisting of two test trials). For the trial blocks using novel objects, there was an exploration phase, a salience phase, a training phase, and a test phase. The basic design of the trial blocks is depicted in Figure 4.

The familiar blocks in all experiments were the first and third blocks in the design. The familiar trial blocks were included both to familiarize

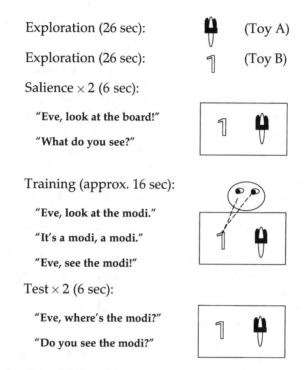

Exploration (26 sec):   (Toy A)

Exploration (26 sec):   (Toy B)

Salience × 2 (6 sec):

"Eve, look at the board!"

"What do you see?"

Training (approx. 16 sec):

"Eve, look at the modi."

"It's a modi, a modi."

"Eve, see the modi!"

Test × 2 (6 sec):

"Eve, where's the modi?"

"Do you see the modi?"

FIGURE 4.—General design of Interactive IPLP: The four phases. Familiar trial blocks contain only exploration and test phases. Novel trial blocks consist of exploration, salience, training, and test phases.

the infants with the test procedure and to assess the validity of the paradigm. Objects in the familiar trial blocks (book, keys, block, and ball) were chosen based on the strong likelihood that even 12-month-old children would have names for these objects in their receptive vocabularies (Fenson et al., 1994). If children demonstrate a looking preference for the requested familiar object, then there is good evidence that they understood what is expected of them in this procedure. The novel trials were the second and fourth blocks in the design. Objects in these trial blocks (e.g., tea strainer, garlic press, bottle opener, etc.) were chosen based on the strong likelihood that 12-month-old children would not have names for these objects in their vocabularies. All speech directed to the children was of the infant-directed variety.

In the *exploration phase* for both the familiar and novel trial blocks, the child was presented, sequentially, with each of two familiar or novel toys in a trial block to play with for 26 s. (The order of presentation was counterbalanced.) This gave the child a chance to have a full range of

35

haptic experience with the objects before the remaining phases and laid the groundwork for subsequent social interaction.

In the *salience phase*, the experimenter hid behind the display board and turned it to reveal the two novel objects side-by-side. Subsequently, the experimenter presented a neutral linguistic stimulus ("Look up here! What do you see?"). This was designed to engage children in the task. After 6 s, the experimenter turned the board (hiding the objects) and stood in preparation for the next phase. Infant looking times to each object provided a baseline measure of their relative salience. In cases where the visual stimuli had been well balanced for perceptual factors, attention (in the form of looking times) should have been evenly distributed between the objects. If the stimuli were intentionally unbalanced on perceptual factors, looking times should have reflected this bias. The experimenter hid behind the board during the salience phase in order to limit the possibility of influencing the child's response.

In the *training phase*, the child saw two objects presented on the table just in front of the display board. The experimenter labeled one of the objects. After getting the child's attention by saying the child's name, the experimenter said, "Horace, look at the modi, the modi. It's a modi." The experiments presented in this *Monograph* manipulate the cues offered during the labeling phase. For example, in some studies, the experimenter varied the social cues used to designate the target object, sometimes using eye gaze alone and, at other times, using pointing, or handling in addition to eye gaze. Language cues were also manipulated: sometimes using words, sometimes using mouth noises (such as clicks) that are not words, and sometimes labeling an object with nonlinguistic noises. Thus, variability in the training phase was key to the test of the hypotheses.

In the *test phase* of both the familiar and novel trial blocks, the experimenter engaged the child when the objects were out of view. For example, the child might have heard, "Where's the modi?" (where "modi" was the name of the targeted object). The experimenter then hid behind the board. The board was flipped over so that the child saw the objects presented on the display board for 6 s. While the objects were visible, the child heard the following linguistic message: "Do you see the X? Look at the X." The board was then turned back over, hiding the objects. This phase was then repeated to obtain an additional assessment of the child's looking times.

The order of presentation of the familiar and novel objects was counterbalanced within each study. For example, in the familiar phases, one child saw the "ball/book" phase first, while another saw the "keys/block" phase. Furthermore, the order of the objects in the exploration phase was also counterbalanced. Thus, one child played with the ball before the block while another played first with the block followed by the ball.

Likewise, the object requested first was also counterbalanced, for example, "ball" first for half and "book" first for half. Finally, the side of presentation was also varied, with the targeted object appearing half the time on the left and half the time on the right. Due to salience issues, the pairing of objects remained constant throughout the studies. Notice, however, that each child was tested on two sets of familiar objects and two sets of novel objects. In this manner, any results seen are not likely to be the result of any specific object-word pairings or specific trial-block effects.

Coding

The video record provided a head-on shot of the infant and a mirror image view of the objects that the infant was examining. Children's visual fixation data during the salience, labeling, and test phases were coded for three things: (a) looks to the right and left at the objects, (b) attention to the experimenter, and (c) looks at neither the objects nor the experimenter.

During the coding process, coders were kept blind to the experimental condition. This was accomplished by covering the portion of the video screen that displayed the objects and experimenter. Thus, all the coders saw was the head-on shot of the infant. In addition, coders were rarely those who administered the original experiment (only 25% of the time) and when they were, they waited 2 weeks in between the live test and the coding. Coders used the Infant Test Timer to calculate infant looking times to the two objects. Only after the coding was complete did the coders check to see which of the toys served as the target object.

To ensure high quality coding in all experiments, observers were trained to become master coders. These coders must not only have reached a criterion level of 90% agreement with other experienced coders, but their own, intrarater reliability must have been above 90% across five consecutive tapes coded twice. Even after they achieved master coder status, 25% of the tapes were subjected to interrater reliability among the master coders in the laboratory. As in previous preferential looking studies, inter- and intrarater reliability was kept above an r value of .90. In fact, the mean interrater reliability was higher (mean $r = .96$).

Independent, Dependent, and Counterbalanced Variables

The dependent variable was mean looking time to the objects in each phase of the experiment. The independent variables changed from experiment to experiment but usually included the age of subjects and one or more experimental manipulations (e.g., direction of experimenter's eye gaze). Variables that were counterbalanced included order of presentation, side of presentation, and the objects used.

Analysis

All analyses across all studies used an alpha level of $p = .05$. In all cases, means were converted to proportion of looking time using the form: target object/(target object + nontarget object), before any analysis was begun. In addition, preliminary analysis of all studies involved between-subjects multivariate analyses of variance (MANOVAs) to check for significant differences due to gender. As these differences were never, in any of the studies, close to significance, gender was therefore excluded from further analysis. Two kinds of primary analysis were used. The first was a one-sample t-test against theoretical chance value of 50% (which would indicate even looking between objects). The second was an analysis of variance (ANOVA) run across phases and between groups.

VALIDATING THE INTERACTIVE IPLP

The crucial test of whether the method works comes from the familiar trial blocks. If infants and toddlers do not look at the target object longer than the nontarget when it is familiar, then there is little hope that researchers can use this procedure to examine novel word learning. Thus, it was imperative to see whether the method could provide valid results. To address this question we combined the data from the familiar trial blocks of all 12 studies reported in this *Monograph*. This provides a kind of meta-analysis of the effectiveness of the procedure based on the familiar trials.

Method

Participants. Children ($N = 338$) were tested at the Temple University Infant Laboratory and the University of Delaware Infant Language Project over 12 separate experiments. Half were male and half were female. There were three age groups. The 12-month-old age group ($n = 242$), ranging in age from 11.26 to 13.89 months ($M = 12.55$, $SD = 0.45$), participated in all 12 studies. The mean number of words in their productive vocabulary was 10.45 with a standard deviation of 11.86. The 19-month-old group ($n = 48$), ranging in age from 18.56 to 20.43 months ($M = 19.48$, $SD = 0.40$), participated in two studies, as did the 24-month-old group ($n = 48$), ranging in age from 23.07 to 27.72 months ($M = 24.52$, $SD = 0.80$). The mean number of words (with standard deviations in parentheses) in their productive vocabularies was 149.41 (147.60) and 333.76 (191.62), respectively.

Procedure and stimuli. The familiar trial blocks were run as described above, as part of 12 separate experiments. The familiar blocks in all experiments were the first and third blocks in the design. The same familiar pairs of stimuli were used across all experiments. The first pair of objects was a brightly colored pink and green ball (4″ in diameter) and a small children's book that was also pink and green (measuring 4″ × 6″). The second pair of objects was a set of multicolored, plastic keys (3″ × 1″) that dangled from a white plastic key ring (3″ in diameter), and a wooden block with alphabet letters on each side (2″ cubed). In addition to familiarity, the objects were chosen because they occupied approximately the same amount of space when velcroed to the display board.

Results

The mean looking time to the targeted and nontargeted familiar objects is presented in Table 1. It shows that for all ages, across all studies, infants looked longer at the targeted object on the familiar trials. The infants' performance in each of the age groups was tested against a theoretical chance level of .50. At all age levels, the proportion of infant looking toward the target object differed significantly from chance. That is, the 12-month-olds, $t(241) = 4.00$, $p < .0001$; 19-month-olds, $t(47) = 5.79$, $p < .0001$; and 24-month-olds, $t(47) = 10.92$, $p < .0001$, all looked proportionately longer at the targeted familiar object.

Discussion

In 12 different studies, with children ranging in age from 12 to 24 months, the method has proven successful. Children consistently look

TABLE 1

MEAN LOOKING TIME (*SD*) IN SECONDS TO FAMILIAR OBJECTS
BY AGE ACROSS ALL STUDIES

	12-month-olds $n = 242$		19-month-olds $n = 48$		24-month-olds $n = 48$	
	M	*SD*	*M*	*SD*	*M*	*SD*
Target	2.77	0.90	3.44	0.87	3.76	0.86
Nontarget	2.34	0.81	1.82	0.65	1.53	0.46
% to Target	54.2*		65.3**		71.1**	

Note.—Planned contrasts against a theoretical chance value of 50% were used, $*p < .05$, $**p < .01$.

longer at the target object than at the nontarget object on the familiar trials. This result suggests that at least for words already in their comprehension vocabulary, children as young as 12 months of age are engaged in the task and can demonstrate their word knowledge. These results are particularly compelling because not all 12-month-old children knew the familiar words. That is, although these words were reported in the vocabulary of over half of these infants (64%, according to parental report), many did not know all of the familiar words. As an added benefit, participant loss—to be reported individually for each study—is well below that traditionally found in methods used with infants. Less than 25% of 12-month-olds, 19-months-olds, and 24-month-olds failed to complete the task. In the chapters that follow, we use this new method to explore the kinds of word learning strategies that infants and toddlers employ as their skill in word learning develops.

IV. LEARNING NOVEL NOUNS: CHILDREN USE MULTIPLE CUES

Rebecca J. Brand

The emergentist coalition model of word learning described in chapter 2 is a hybrid model that builds on and extends the developmental lexical principles framework (Golinkoff et al., 1994). This model of word learning (Hollich et al., 1998; Golinkoff, Hirsh-Pasek, & Hollich, 1999; Hirsh-Pasek, Golinkoff, & Hollich, in press) offers the child multiple cues to attach a novel label to a novel object. As the research reviewed above has demonstrated, children may use social, attentional, and language cues to learn new words. Unlike experiments conducted in the laboratory that manipulate single cues, the same word learning situation, in the real world, may offer combinations of these cues. The emergentist coalition model embraces this complexity, incorporating the full range of cues to word learning, investigating both individual cues as well as how the cues interact with each other.

The developmental cast of this model makes it imperative to study the origins of word learning as well as the transformation that takes place in the 2nd year of life. Now with a method that can investigate development of language in 12- and 24-month-old children, data needed to be collected that assessed the three main hypotheses of the model: (a) that children detect and utilize multiple cues for word learning, (b) that their reliance on these cues changes over the course of development, and (c) that these principles for word learning emerge from the word learning experience.

OVERVIEW OF EXPERIMENTS 1–3 AND HYPOTHESES

This chapter presents the first series of experiments designed to test these hypotheses. Children at three ages were studied in the Interactive IPLP: 12- to 13-month-olds just at the beginning of word learning; 19- to 20-month-olds who may or may not have yet experienced a vocabulary spurt; and 24- to 25-month-olds who typically have sizeable production vocabularies. Experiment 1 was designed to assess the utility of the Inter-active IPLP and to examine whether, and under what conditions, children at these three ages can learn a novel word. Experiment 2 was a control experiment designed to explore the magnitude of the word learning effects found in Experiment 1. Experiment 3 offered a further control and a critical test of whether 12-month-olds had really learned novel words in Experiment 1.

Hypothesis 1: Children Are Sensitive to Multiple Cues in Word Learning

The studies presented in this chapter investigated two of the cues in the coalition of word learning cues: attentional and social. In particular, we wanted to see whether both attention-getting cues, such as perceptual salience, and social cues, such as eye gaze, were available to infants in the word learning situation. Perceptual salience was manipulated by using two objects of unequal salience. The "interesting" object was brightly colored and had moving parts. The "boring" object was dull beige and did not have moving parts. By creating these two dramatically different objects, we hoped to produce a situation in which one object would receive a greater amount of attention than the other object receives. Social eye gaze was crossed with perceptual salience by creating two conditions (similar to Baldwin, 1995). In the *coincidental* condition, the highly attractive object was the focus of the experimenter's eye gaze during the training phase. Hence, the two cues were "coincident" with each other, both highlighting the same object. In the conflict condition, the boring object was the focus of the experiment's gaze during training. In this manner, the two cues were at odds with each other, each cue highlighting a different object.

Could children show us that they were aware of both kinds of word learning cues, attentional and social? Would they follow the experimenter's gaze to the target object during training—even in the conflict condition when the experimenter looked more at the more boring object? Could children's responses indicate which cue they weighted more heavily, salience or eye gaze? Could infants learn a label for the object indicated by eye gaze, even when perceptual salience favored the interesting object in the conflict condition? We predicted that the two older groups would provide clear evidence of having detected both of these word learning cues by following the experimenter's gaze during training and by showing subsequent evidence of word learning on the test trials, even in the more difficult conflict condition. A subsidiary question was whether 12-month-olds could use both kinds of cues. Would they follow another's gaze to a focal point in the context? We predicted that the youngest children would note both types of cues but only the cue of perceptual salience would be used in the service of word learning.

Hypothesis 2: The Relative Weightings of the Cues for
Word Learning Shift With Word Learning Experience

Consistent with the emergentist coalition model, we also predicted that 12-month-olds should be more influenced by attentional cues when attaching a word to a referent than by social cues. In fact, we predicted that the younger group would affix the novel word to the most interesting object regardless of condition, on the assumption that the relative weighting of cues favor attentional cues (such as perceptual salience) at the beginning of word learning. We further hypothesized that older children might use even subtle social cues, such as eye gaze, relatively more than perceptual salience and would "read" the speaker's intent when affixing a label to a referent, even when the target object is the more boring alternative.

Hypothesis 3: Children Move From an Immature
to a Mature Principle of Reference

In the 2nd year of life, the course of word learning is characterized by a dramatic shift: First, only words that coincide with one's own perspective are learned; then words are learned from the perspective of the speaker. The prediction that older children will use social cues relatively more than perceptual salience to connect words with referents, and that younger children will do just the opposite, suggests that these children are approaching word learning in a fundamentally different way. Young children, although sensitive to a coalition of cues for word learning, may not know which of the many cues in the coalition can be relied on for word learning. In the present context, younger children may reveal their uncertainty about the role that social cues play in word learning. The consequence of being unsure about the merit of different cues is that the learner may be conservative and require converging data to form word-referent connections (as Baldwin, 1993, has found at later ages). Children with an immature principle of reference might need to have multiple, overlapping cues for word-referent mapping relative to children with a mature principle of reference.

EXPERIMENT 1. THE PRINCIPLE OF REFERENCE: AFFIXING A NOVEL WORD TO A REFERENT

The purpose of this experiment was to explore whether children could learn novel words in the Interactive IPLP when the cues of perceptual salience and social eye gaze either coincided or were pitted against each other. Social cues like eye gaze and gesture often work together to indicate which of the many objects in the scene the speaker is labeling. In contrast, perceptual salience—whether an object is brightly colored, interestingly shaped, or moving—is less reliable and informative for discovering which object is the referent of a novel label. For example, a young child who hears a mother's telephone conversation about autos might incorrectly attach the label "car" to the object he is playing with. Conversely, in the case where the mother labels the car while the child is looking at it, social and attentional cues combine to provide the optimal learning environment.

We predicted that when the cues for word learning were redundant and both "pointed" to the same object, word learning should be less demanding than when these cues were put into conflict. That is, when a speaker used her eye gaze to indicate that the most salient object in the environment was the one being labeled, word learning should have been relatively easy. When a speaker, however, used eye gaze to indicate that the object being labeled is the more boring, and *not* the more interesting object, word learning should have been relatively more difficult. In this manner, putting word learning cues in conflict should present a puzzle for young children who are not yet sure how to weight the cues for word learning. Older children should learn novel words in accord with eye gaze, but they should still show some effects of stimulus salience.

These claims are consonant with findings from the joint attention literature. Furthermore, they may help us understand why attention-following (when the adult names what the child is focused on) is more effective for word learning than attention-switching (when the adult names an object the child is not already looking at), as in Dunham et al. (1993). When cues are in conflict—as they are when the child is attending to one object and the adult is labeling another—the child must shift attention and look at the less interesting object, both of which serve to weaken the bond between word and object. This conflict would be especially pronounced when, as is predicted by the emergentist coalition model, children are not sure how to weight the various cues available for word learning. The present study allows us to evaluate whether the lure of object salience overwhelms the cue of social eye gaze in a word learning situation for children at three different ages in the 2nd year of life.

Pairs of objects were selected in which one object was far more attractive than the other one was. For example, one pair consisted of a white bottle opener and a pink and orange clacker that could make a noise if shaken vigorously. In the coincidental condition, the toy that coincided with children's salience preferences—the interesting toy (in this case, the clacker)—was labeled. If children are using both social eye gaze and perceptual salience, they should learn best in this condition where the cues are in alignment. In the conflict condition, the toy that did not coincide with the children's preferences—the boring toy (the bottle opener)—was labeled.

The conflict condition presents the clearest test of the cues children rely on in word learning since the cues are in competition. Children with a mature principle of reference should respond differently in this condition than children with an immature principle of reference. Thus, the older groups were expected to learn the novel words but still show the effects of stimulus salience. As 12-month-olds are expected to have an immature principle of reference, we predicted that they would attach the novel labels, regardless of condition, to the interesting object.

Three questions were of interest:

1. Were the objects we considered salient actually salient to the children?

2. Did children of all ages follow eye gaze in training, which would indicate that eye gaze could be detected?

3. Did children use eye gaze in the service of word learning? That is, did they use eye gaze in assigning the referent to the novel label even in the difficult conflict condition?

Method

Participants. Thirty-two children at each of three ages (half boys and half girls) composed the final sample ($N = 96$). A total of 58 additional participants (37%) were lost due to fussiness and experimenter error. Half of the children were tested in the Delaware laboratory; half were tested in the Temple laboratory. The age range for the youngest group of 12-month-olds was 11.59 to 13.16 ($M = 12.53$, $SD = 0.428$); for the 19-month-old group, 19.05 to 20.43 ($M = 19.504$, $SD = 0.430$); and for the 24-month-olds, 23.07 to 27.72 ($M = 24.591$, $SD = 0.908$).

Stimuli. The objects selected for the study were small household objects thought to be unfamiliar to the infants. Two objects were selected because of their bright colors and ability to move (a blue gel- and silver sparkle-filled wand, and an orange and pink party clacker.) These interesting objects were hypothesized to be highly salient to the children. Two "boring" objects were selected due to their dull colors and drab appearance (a white cabinet latch and a beige bottle opener). The interesting wand was paired with the boring latch, and the party clacker was paired with the bottle opener. In this manner, we created two pairs of objects whose perceptual salience was dramatically dissimilar. Two novel labels were also chosen, "modi" and "dawnoo."

Procedure. Children were randomly assigned to be in either the conflict or coincidental condition for both novel trial blocks. As described in chapter 3, this experiment used the standard design (see Figure 4, in chapter 3). Thus, for the two trial blocks on which novel objects were used, an exploration phase (26 s with each object) was followed by a test trial with "neutral" linguistic stimuli to assess stimulus salience (6 s). In the training trials that followed, the experimenter labeled the target object five times while looking at it, and then, while hidden from view, tested for learning of the label with two test trials in which the target was requested by name. In the coincidental condition, the interesting toy was labeled, via eye gaze. In the conflict condition, the boring toy was labeled, via eye gaze. The labels were counterbalanced across trials.

Results

Table 2 depicts the mean looking times to the interesting and boring objects in the two conditions (coincidental and conflict) at all phases (salience, training, and test) and age levels (12, 19, and 24 months) for this experiment (as well as for Experiment 2). It also shows the mean proportion of time infant gaze is fixed on the interesting object. Any proportion of greater than 50 indicates preferential looking to the interesting object. A proportion of less than 50 indicates preferential looking to the boring object. For example, in the coincidental condition for the 12-month-olds, the percentage of attention allocated to the interesting object during salience was 65.1. Table 2 also displays the change in this looking proportion between the coincidental and conflict conditions (percentage change). This provides a measure of the effectiveness of the experimental manipulation.

Overall analysis. A mixed 3 (phase: salience/training/test) × 2 (condition: conflict/coincidental) × 2 (age: 12/19/24 months) ANOVA was run. It yielded a significant main effect of phase, $F(2, 180) = 4.956$, $MSE = 0.086$; a significant main effect of condition, $F(1, 180) = 42.833$, $MSE = 1.113$; a significant main effect of age, $F(2, 180) = 3.123$, $MSE = 0.081$; a significant phase-by-condition interaction, $F(2, 180) = 30.168$, $MSE = 0.526$; as well as a significant phase-by-age-by-condition interaction, $F(4, 180) = 4.214$, $MSE = 0.073$. To decompose these effects we analyzed each phase separately.[1]

Salience trials. Were the toys of unequal salience? Our intuitions about differential object salience were validated. Children spent, on average, 2.5

[1]According to Keppel (1991), this approach is advisable. This decision was made a priori directly from our hypothesis as in Coldren and Columbo (1994).

more s looking at the interesting toy. A between-subjects ANOVA conducted to ascertain if there were any differences between age groups yielded nonsignificant results, $F(2, 93) = 0.579$, $MSE = 0.012$. Therefore the results were pooled to test against a theoretical chance level of .50. Indeed, infants at all ages looked proportionately more at the object we considered interesting, $t(95) = 10.166$, $p < .0001$. Furthermore, a large effect size was observed ($d = 1.03$).

Training trials. Did participants follow the experimenter's gaze during training trials? Because one of the objects was intentionally more interesting than the other, there is no reason. a priori, to suppose infants should look proportionately longer at the trained object, even if they were following the experimenter's eye gaze. Instead, the critical criterion for an effect of gaze is to be found in a distinction between the conflict and coincidental conditions. In each of these conditions, infants heard and saw exactly the same events. The only difference was that in the conflict condition, the experimenter was looking in one direction (at the boring toy), and in the coincidental condition, the experimenter was looking in the other direction (at the interesting toy). Thus, the relevant data are found in the percentage change row of Table 2.

A between-subjects 2 (condition: conflict/coincidental) × 2 (age: 12/ 19/24 months) ANOVA was run on the training trial. It yielded a significant main effect of condition, $F(1, 90) = 63.949$, $MSE = 1.630$; and a significant condition-by-age interaction, $F(2, 90) = 11.032$, $MSE = .281$. Subsequent Scheffe's post hoc tests demonstrated that these effects were due to a significant condition effect for the 19- and 24-month-olds (critical difference = .065, 19-month-old mean difference = .334, and 24-month-old mean difference = .4) and an absence of an effect for the 12-month-olds. Thus, in the conflict condition, the youngest group did not follow the experimenter to the boring object, preferring instead to gaze an equal proportion of the time at the interesting object, in both conditions. The middle age group did look longer at the boring object in the conflict condition than in the coincidental. Finally, the older group was also quite successful in following the experimenter's gaze to the boring toy in the conflict condition. Indeed, in a test against a chance level of 50%, 24-month-old infants looked proportionately longer at the boring object, $t(15) = 4.030$, $p = .0005$. This was true of the 19-month-olds as well, $t(15) = 2.474$, $p = .0129$.

Test trials. Did infants demonstrate evidence of word learning during the test trials? Evidence that the novel names had been learned would be found if the amount of time children spent looking at the interesting toy in the conflict condition significantly differed from the time spent looking

TABLE 2

Experiments 1 and 2: Mean Looking Time (*SD*) in Seconds as a Function of Phase, Age Group, and Condition

	Salience	Training	Test
Experiment 1 (Perceptual Salience and Eye Gaze)			
12-month-olds			
Coincidental			
Interesting	3.73 (0.77)	4.60 (2.71)	2.95 (0.90)
Boring	2.00 (0.85)	2.02 (1.25)	1.34 (0.58)
% to Int.	65.1**	69.4**	68.7**
Conflict			
Interesting	3.81 (1.32)	4.64 (3.35)	2.83 (0.86)
Boring	1.58 (0.84)	2.32 (1.28)	1.47 (0.50)
% to Int.	70.6**	66.6**	65.8**
Difference			
% Change	−5.5	2.8	2.9
19-month-olds			
Coincidental			
Interesting	3.37 (0.76)	5.66 (2.21)	3.65 (0.75)
Boring	2.35 (0.81)	1.96 (0.89)	1.28 (0.42)
% to Int.	58.9**	74.3**	74.0**
Conflict			
Interesting	3.89 (0.97)	2.68 (1.98)	2.66 (0.75)
Boring	1.94 (0.79)	3.54 (1.63)	2.04 (0.69)
% to Int.	66.7**	43.0*	56.6*
Difference			
% Change	−7.8	31.3**	17.4**
24-month-olds			
Coincidental			
Interesting	3.58 (0.99)	6.78 (3.04)	3.49 (0.94)
Boring	2.12 (0.91)	2.01 (1.10)	1.73 (0.70)
% to Int.	62.8**	77.1**	66.9**
Conflict			
Interesting	3.85 (0.59)	2.70 (1.33)	2.49 (1.08)
Boring	2.02 (0.51)	4.22 (1.26)	2.85 (0.85)
% to Int.	65.6**	39.0**	46.6*
Difference			
% Change	−2.8	38.1**	20.3**

continued

at that same toy in the coincidental condition. These data can be seen in the percentage change row of Table 2. That is, similar to the argument in the training trials above, even if the children looked a majority of the time at the interesting object, any difference in looking times between the conditions must indicate the impact of the social cues offered during training. Thus, this analysis asked whether children looked proportionately

TABLE 2—*Continued*

	Salience	Training	Test
Experiment 2 (Perceptual Salience, Eye Gaze, and Switched Sides at Test)			
12-month-olds			
Coincidental			
Interesting	4.38 (0.66)	5.65 (2.01)	3.12 (0.41)
Boring	1.27 (0.49)	1.54 (1.31)	1.56 (0.58)
% to Int.	77.5**	78.6**	66.7**
Conflict			
Interesting	3.17 (0.87)	4.21 (1.95)	3.02 (0.72)
Boring	2.25 (0.74)	2.31 (1.29)	1.80 (0.50)
% to Int.	58.4**	64.6**	62.7**
Difference			
% Change	19.1**	14.0**	4.0
19-month-olds			
Coincidental			
Interesting	3.27 (0.64)	6.29 (1.65)	2.84 (1.40)
Boring	2.29 (0.71)	2.03 (1.98)	1.57 (0.41)
% to Int.	58.8*	75.6**	64.3*
Conflict			
Interesting	3.61 (0.61)	3.68 (2.39)	2.85 (0.84)
Boring	1.72 (0.72)	4.12 (1.98)	1.66 (0.47)
% to Int.	67.8**	47.1	63.2**
Difference			
% Change	−9.0	28.5**	1.1
24-month-olds			
Coincidental			
Interesting	3.51 (0.82)	5.91 (2.49)	3.93 (1.29)
Boring	1.97 (0.84)	1.92 (0.67)	1.19 (0.64)
% to Int.	64.1**	75.5**	76.8**
Conflict			
Interesting	3.96 (0.91)	2.90 (1.10)	2.62 (0.59)
Boring	1.96 (1.00)	4.11 (0.92)	2.34 (0.74)
% to Int.	66.9**	41.4*	52.8
Difference			
% Change	−2.8	34.1**	24.3**

Note.—Planned contrasts against a theoretical chance value of 50% for the % to Int. and against a theoretical difference of 0 for the % Change, respectively, were used, $*p < .05$, $**p < .01$.

longer at the interesting toy in the coincidental condition when it was asked for by name than they looked at that same toy when it appeared in the conflict condition when it was not requested.

A between-subjects 2 (condition: conflict/coincidental) × 2 (age: 12/19/24 months) ANOVA was conducted. It yielded a significant main effect of condition, $F(1, 90) = 34.046$, $MSE = 0.508$; a significant main effect of age, $F(2, 90) = 3.681$, $MSE = 0.055$; and a significant condition-by-age interaction, $F(2, 90) = 4.087$, $MSE = 0.061$. Subsequent Scheffe's post hoc tests demonstrated that these effects were again due to a significant condition effect for the 19- and 24-month-olds (critical difference = .05, 19-month-old mean difference = .17, and 24-month-old mean difference = .218), and an absence of an effect for the 12-month-olds (mean difference = .048).

Thus, the youngest children seemed unaffected by condition, as they did not look at the interesting toy longer when it was requested than when it was not. By 19 months, however, children showed an effect of the cue of eye gaze on word learning. In test trials, they looked at the interesting object significantly more in the coincidental condition when it was requested than in the conflict condition when it was not requested. That 19-month-old youngsters are still influenced by perceptual salience, however, is indicated by the fact that they still look at the interesting toy the majority of the time in both conditions. In contrast, by 24 months of age, children look at the boring object significantly longer in the conflict condition. A direct comparison of the 19- and 24-month-olds revealed a significant difference in the proportion of time these two age groups spent looking at the interesting object in the conflict condition, $t(33) = 2.15$, $p = .03$. This finding suggests that social eye gaze was weighted more heavily by 24 months of age.

Discussion

Experiment 1 revealed varied patterns of word learning in children at three different ages. Both the 19- and the 24-month-olds provided us with data that multiple cues, perceptual salience and social eye gaze, influenced their word learning. Despite strong salience preferences, children in these two older groups followed the experimenter's gaze to the target object in both conditions, during the training trials. In the test trials, while both groups showed sensitivity to eye gaze, the lure of object salience was greater for the 19-month-olds. That is, despite a significant condition effect, the 19-month-olds still showed the effect of perceptual salience by looking relatively more at the attractive object during test trials in both conditions. This suggests that their word learning was not quite as strong as that of the older group, in which 24-month-olds looked significantly longer at the boring object during test trials of the conflict condition.

What about the 12-month-olds? From this experiment, it appears that 12-month-olds were not sensitive to eye gaze but only to perceptual salience. This strong experimental manipulation, however, which placed the two cues in conflict, may have masked the abilities of the youngest group. It is unclear if the 12-month-olds were insensitive to the speaker's use of eye gaze because the task demands were so weighted in favor of perceptual salience. It is, therefore, impossible to conclude whether the youngest group was using multiple cues. In fact, it is difficult to know whether the youngest group learned a novel label at all. Regardless of condition and experimental phase (training and test), these infants could have been simply looking at their favorite object. Thus, for this age group, there is no evidence of word learning in this task.

Nonetheless, this experiment provides evidence that between 12, 19, and 24 months of age there is a shift toward relying on social eye gaze. This is supported by the fact that 24-month-olds were looking longer at the boring object during test, the significant age-by-condition interaction, and the stepwise increases in the proportion of looking toward the boring object observed between the age groups in the conflict condition. It was as if children came to realize, over time, that perceptual salience was not as reliable a cue for word learning as social eye gaze. By 24 months, children recognized that although there may be a large discrepancy in the attractiveness of the objects present during labeling, what matters for word learning was which object the speaker intends to label. Social eye gaze was thus weighted more heavily at 24 months than it was at 12 months of age.

Support for this idea also comes from a study by Moore et al. (1999). Reasoning as we do that the way to discover whether children are in tune with the referential intentions of the speaker is to put cues into competition, they created a situation with two objects of differential salience on either side of the speaker. Either the experimenter turned to and labeled the attractive moving object (the static object remained in view), or the experimenter turned to and labeled the boring, static object while the non-target object (still in view) was moving. The question was whether 18- and 24-month-olds would rely on the referential intentions of the speaker as signaled by eye gaze or whether they would rely on perceptual salience in affixing the label. As in our experiment, the 24-month-olds had no difficulty learning the label of the target object, even when it was the more boring alternative. The 18-month-olds, however, did not learn a label when the experimenter named the boring object but only when the experimenter named the interesting object. This finding suggests that 18-month-old word learning is still very fragile.

EXPERIMENT 2: THE FRAGILITY OF EARLY WORD LEARNING: CHANGING THE SIDES OF THE OBJECTS AT TEST

Experiment 2 had two purposes. The first was to assess the fragility of word learning, even with children at the two older ages. Could they still find the target they had been trained on if it changed sides during the test trials? Although it is standard in infant paradigms to counterbalance the side of the target objects at test, training side and test side remained constant in Experiment 1 to see whether infants could learn a new word in the best of circumstances. Even spatial changes are known to increase task difficulty. We predicted that the 24-month-olds would show a continued ability to locate the target even when it was placed in a new position at test. As the 19-month-olds were still influenced by stimulus salience, however, it might be the case that relocating the target object would require an attention switch that they would find difficult.

The second reason to conduct this study was to rule out an artifact. Could it be that the children in the two older groups were tracking the sides of the objects and then, taking their cue from the training trial, assuming that the experimenter was requesting the target side rather than the target object with the label?

Method

Participants. Sixteen children at each of three ages (half boys and half girls) composed the final sample ($N = 48$). A total of 22 additional participants (31%) were lost due to fussiness and experimenter error. The age range for the 12-month-olds was 11.53 to 13.49 ($M = 12.426$, $SD = 0.516$). For 19-month-olds, the range was 18.56 to 20.1 ($M = 19.504$, $SD = 0.347$); for the 24-month-olds, the range was 23.56 to 25.1 ($M = 24.369$, $SD = 0.518$).

Procedure. Children were randomly assigned to be in either the conflict or coincidental condition. This experiment used the same procedure as in Experiment 1, except for the fact that the objects switched their positions on the test trials.

Results

Again, Table 2 depicts the mean looking times to the boring and interesting objects in the two conditions at all phases and age levels, as well as the proportion of looking time and percentage change of this proportion across conditions. It shows that at all ages the infants replicated closely the effects seen in the previous experiment, until the test trials when the objects switched sides. The test trials looking times were very different from Experiment 1. In this study, however, the 12-month-olds *did* show evidence of noticing social cues during the training trials.

Overall analysis. A mixed 3 (phase: salience/training/test) × 2 (condition: conflict/coincidental) × 2 (age: 12/19/24 months) ANOVA was run.

It yielded a significant main effect of condition, $F(1, 84) = 17.864$, $MSE = 0.379$; a significant main effect of age, $F(2, 84) = 4.811$, $MSE = 0.102$; a significant phase-by-condition interaction, $F(2, 84) = 14.836$, $MSE = 0.255$; as well as a significant phase-by-age-by-condition interaction, $F(4, 84) = 3.257$, $MSE = .056$. To decompose these effects, we analyzed each phase separately as in Experiment 1.

Salience trials. Were the toys of unequal salience? Our intuitions about differential object salience were again validated. A between-subjects ANOVA run to ascertain if there were any differences between age groups yielded nonsignificant results, $F(2, 45) = 1.192$, $MSE = 0.024$. Therefore, the results were pooled to test against a theoretical chance level of .50. Infants at all ages looked proportionately more ($M = .680$, $SD = .142$) at the object we considered interesting, $t(48) = 8.782$, $p < .0001$. Furthermore, the results seen were not simply due to increased power due to a large number of participants. A large effect size was again observed ($d = 1.26$), suggesting these results would be seen for much smaller numbers as well.

Training trials. Did participants follow the experimenter's gaze during training trials? The pattern found in Experiment 1 was replicated with all age groups. A between-subjects 2 (condition: conflict/coincidental) × 3 (age: 12/19/24 months) ANOVA was run. It yielded a significant main effect of condition, $F(1, 42) = 42.432$, $MSE = 0.764$; a significant main effect of age, $F(2, 42) = 6.483$, $MSE = 0.117$; and a significant condition-by-age interaction, $F(2, 42) = 3.579$, $MSE = 0.064$. Subsequent Scheffe's post hoc tests demonstrated that these effects were due to significant condition effect at all ages (critical difference = .078, 12-month-old mean difference = .121, 19-month-old mean difference = .374, and 24-month-old mean difference = .261), as well as a significant age effect between all groups. Thus, children at all ages, even 12 months, appeared to distinguish eye gaze direction, performing differently in the conflict and coincidental conditions, but children at the older ages performed better.

Test trials. Did infants demonstrate evidence of word learning during the test trials? As in the previous experiment, because of large salience differences between the objects, the key comparison was in how much attention is allocated to the interesting object in the conflict versus the coincidental conditions. Any change in relative attention to the interesting object can only be attributed to the differential social cues provided by the experimenter.

A between-subjects 2 (condition: conflict/coincidental) × 2 (age: 12/19/24 months) ANOVA was run. It yielded a significant main effect of condition, $F(1, 42) = 6.046$, $MSE = 0.106$; and a trend toward a significant condition-by-age interaction, $F(2, 42) = 2.805$, $MSE = 0.049$, $p = .071$. Subsequent Scheffe's post hoc tests demonstrated that these effects were due to a significant condition effect for the 24-month-olds (critical difference = .077, 24-month-old mean difference = .261) and an absence of an effect for the other groups (12-month-old mean difference = .05, 19-month-old mean difference = .012). As the percentage change row of Table 2 shows, 12- and 19-month-olds were unable to conclusively demonstrate word learning when the toys changed sides during the test trials. That is, neither a difference of 4.0% nor of 1.1% between the conflict and coincidental conditions supports the conclusion that word learning occurred in this more difficult task. The 24-month-olds show a different pattern. They do show a significant difference between conditions (as manifested in the significant difference in attention to the interesting object across conditions). The 24.3% difference (as seen in Table 2) indicates that 24-month-olds were still sensitive to social cues in the mapping of word to object.

Discussion

In Experiment 2, we examined the durability of early word learning. Would children, after hearing a novel name only five times, find the target object when it changed sides at test? Given that 19-month-olds' responses were dominated by sensitivity to perceptual salience, we thought that perhaps this manipulation would tax their word learning skills. We also wished to see whether we could rule out a potential methodological artifact. Could we find any evidence—at least from the oldest group— that children could still find the target when it changed sides during the test trials?

The data indicated that the 24-month-olds were partially resistant to this new manipulation. Thus, they continued to show an effect of condition even when the target changed sides during the test trials. That is, although they did not look significantly longer at the boring object during test in the conflict condition (as compared to the interesting object), their proportion of looking to the objects did significantly change between conditions. Thus, the 24-month-olds did look significantly more at the boring object (and less at the interesting object) in the conflict condition than in the coincidental condition. This is revealed in the percentage change row of Table 2. For this reason, we can tentatively conclude that the 24-month-olds are proficient to the point that spatial changes in the location of the target object can be partially overcome. In addition, the fact that 24-month-olds partially follow the switch of the target objects at test indicates that the method is not simply tapping children's desire to continue watching the side where training took place. After all, if this explanation were true, the oldest group should have been insistent about remaining on the same side and not followed the target object across the switch. Instead, the Interactive IPLP seems to tap the processes involved in genuine word learning.

By contrast, 19-month-olds did not prove quite as expert. In comparison to Experiment 1, they became confused when the target changed sides and did not show an effect of condition. That is, they looked significantly longer at the interesting object in both the coincidental and conflict conditions. Combining the present results with those of Moore et al. (1999) indicates that the poor performance seen in the 19-month-olds is probably not attributable to problems in methodology. Rather, it seems that, in 19-month-olds, word learning is still quite fragile. Possibly if the 19-month-olds had had more exposures to the novel name and the target (particularly if this exposure included switching sides), then this switch would not have been a problem. In the real world, it is unlikely that objects have to be seen in exactly the same context and spatial location by 19 months of age for children to recognize their labels. Then again, objects tend to be labeled across many contexts and locations as well. Perhaps the experience of hearing a novel label used for multiple exemplars across multiple contexts is critical to 19-month-old word learning (Hollich, 1999; see also Akhtar & Montague, 1999). In any case, the fact that the switch caused confusion for the 19-month-olds is telling. Factors not quite relevant to word learning—such as spatial location and object salience (Moore et al., 1999)—can still intrude on the word learning process. The development evinced by the 19-month-olds in Experiment 1, while impressive, is still not as firm as that shown 5 months later by the 24-month-olds. For 24-month-olds, the speaker's referential intent is apparently taken into consideration.

Nonetheless, from the first two experiments, we are left with a question of how to best characterize the 12-month-olds' word learning. Recall that we had predicted that 12-month-olds would be in possession of an immature principle of reference, learning words only from their own point of view and needing multiple cues to be in alignment. We predicted that for the youngest group, the novel word would be associated with the most interesting object, regardless of what the speaker labeled. Although no firm conclusions can be drawn with respect to the 12-month-old data in Experiments 1 or 2, the data from those experiments are not inconsistent with this prediction. Although some evidence of 12-month-old sensitivity to eye gaze was seen in the training trials of Experiment 2, in all test trials, 12-month-olds paid significantly more attention to the interesting than to the boring toy, regardless of condition. Perhaps perceptual salience is so compelling for 12-month-olds that it is the only cue that matters in attaching a label.

Alternatively, the 12-month-olds might have failed to attach a label at all. Perhaps they looked at the toy they preferred, ignoring the fact that a label was being offered. This lower-level explanation of their behavior could not be ruled out in the context of Experiments 1 and 2. In order to see if these youngsters had attached the novel names to the interesting object in both conditions, a subsequent experiment (Experiment 3) was performed. This experiment also allowed us to disambiguate the type of reference 12-month-olds possess and to see how best to characterize the course of lexical development.

EXPERIMENT 3: TWELVE-MONTH-OLDS ARE SENSITIVE TO SOCIAL EYE GAZE AND OBJECT SALIENCE IN LEARNING NOVEL NAMES

To evaluate whether the 12-month-olds had attached the label to the interesting object, regardless of condition, or whether they were merely attending to the object they found most attractive, an additional group of 12-month-olds was brought into the laboratory and run through a slightly altered experimental design. Borrowing from Oviatt (1980), in this design, the test phase was now followed by two additional phases. In the first of these additional phases, called the "new phase," the experimenter requested a different label even though the same items were presented on the board. For example, if the children had been trained and tested on the word, "modi," the experimenter now asked the child to find the "dawnoo." The logic of this phase was as follows. If the original word, "modi" had been successfully paired with the target object, then the introduction of the novel word ("dawnoo") should draw the child's attention away from the target object. This is because a new label would disrupt the previously established pairing. In contrast, if the children simply like to look at the interesting toy, then the introduction of the novel label should make no difference. Children should continue to look at the interesting object. In the second additional phase, called the "recovery phase," the experimenter again requested the modi. If the child had originally paired the label "modi" with the target object, then the reintroduction of this label should create renewed attention to the original target item. This would indicate that boredom was not responsible for any changes in looking preference seen in the prior phase. Thus, in the two additional phases, we anticipated a pattern of responding such that infants who looked at the target object during the test phase would look away from the target object during the new phase and back to the target in the recovery phase. This pattern of results could only appear if the original label made a difference. Furthermore, if there was a significant effect of condition, then we could conclude that these children were sensitive to social cues and that these cues influence children's mapping.

Method

Participants. Thirty-two children (half boys and half girls) composed the final sample. The age range was 12.03 to 13.43 ($M = 12.69$, $SD = 0.281$). A total of 13 additional participants (28%) were lost due to fussiness and experimenter error.

Procedure and stimuli. For each block of trials, children saw the same toys and experienced the same sequence of trials, as in Experiment 1 and 2, through the test phase. Two additional phases then occurred. On the first, called the "new phase," a new label was used, while the same toys were presented. On the second, called the "recovery phase," the original name was again used.

Results

Overall analysis. Table 3 depicts the mean looking times to the boring and interesting objects in the two conditions for all phases, as well as the proportion of looking to the interesting object and the percentage change in this proportion between conditions. A mixed 5 (phase: salience/training/test/new/recovery) × 2 (condition: conflict/coincidental) ANOVA was run. It yielded a significant main effect of phase, $F(4, 120) = 7.405$, $MSE = 0.10$; and a significant phase-by-condition interaction, $F(4, 120) = 3.844$, $MSE = 0.057$. To decompose these effects, we analyzed each set of trials separately as in the previous experiments.

TABLE 3

EXPERIMENT 3 (PERCEPTUAL SALIENCE AND EYE GAZE—MODIFIED DESIGN):
MEAN LOOKING TIME (SD) IN SECONDS AS A FUNCTION OF PHASE

	Salience	Training	Test	New	Recovery
Coincidental					
Interesting	3.92 (0.84)	5.40 (1.42)	3.89 (0.88)	2.68 (0.86)	3.48 (1.20)
Boring	1.80 (0.80)	2.40 (1.43)	1.33 (0.63)	2.02 (0.68)	1.19 (0.73)
% to Int.	68.5**	69.2**	74.5**	57.0	74.5**
Conflict					
Interesting	4.34 (0.70)	4.20 (1.52)	4.07 (0.48)	3.17 (0.70)	3.18 (0.48)
Boring	1.36 (0.60)	3.05 (1.93)	1.20 (0.55)	1.57 (0.87)	1.26 (0.73)
% to Int.	76.1**	57.9	77.2**	66.9*	71.6**
Difference					
% Change	−7.6	11.3*	−2.7	−9.9	2.9

Note.—Planned contrasts against a theoretical chance value of 50% for the % to Int. and against a theoretical difference of 0 for the % Change, respectively, were used, *$p < .05$, **$p < .01$.

57

Salience trials. Were the toys of unequal salience? A between-subjects ANOVA run to ascertain if there were any differences between the two conditions yielded nonsignificant results, $F(1, 30) = 0.961$, $MSE = 0.016$. Therefore, the results were pooled to test against a theoretical chance level of .50. Infants looked proportionately more ($M = .710$, $SD = .129$) at the object we considered interesting than at the boring object, $t(31) = 9.226$, $p < .0001$. A large effect size was again observed ($d = 1.65$).

Training trials. Did participants follow the experimenter's gaze during training trials? The pattern found in Experiment 2 was replicated. A between-subjects ANOVA was run. It yielded a significant main effect of condition, $F(1, 30) = 5.93$, $MSE = 0.121$ (see the percentage change row of Table 3). Thus, 12-month-olds again appeared to distinguish eye gaze direction, in that they looked at the two items indiscriminately in the conflict condition but primarily at the interesting object in the coincidental condition.

Test trials. Did infants demonstrate an effect of the label during the test trials? As Table 3 shows, children responded in the test trials just as they had done in Experiment 1 and 2; they looked at the interesting toy significantly longer than they looked at the boring toy, regardless of condition. The true test of whether labeling occurred, however, is to be found in their pattern of responding across the test phase, the new phase, and the recovery phase.

A mixed model 3 (phase: test/new/recovery) × 2 (condition: conflict/coincidental) ANOVA was run. It yielded a significant main effect of phase, $F(2, 90) = 10.179$, $MSE = 0.184$; and a trend toward an effect of condition, $F(1, 90) = 3.945$, $MSE = 0.071$, $p = .05$. Subsequent Scheffe's post hoc tests demonstrated that these effects were due to significant differences between the new phase and all other phases in the coincidental condition (critical difference = .134, test vs. new mean difference = .178, recovery vs. new mean difference = .157. In the conflict condition, there was no significant drop in looking time from the test to new phase (Scheffe's critical difference = .105, mean difference = .104) and no subsequent return in mean looking time to the interesting toy on the recovery phase (mean difference = .078).

Discussion

The purpose of Experiment 3 was to distinguish between two possible interpretations of the 12-month-olds' responses in Experiments 1 and 2. Were the 12-month-olds just looking at the interesting object such that the experimenter's label was irrelevant to the children during all phases?

Alternatively, had children noticed the label and paired the original label with the target object? The clearest interpretation of Experiment 3 is that children noticed the change in labels between the test and new phases. Less clear is whether infants actually attached the original label to the target object. Two pieces of evidence suggest that the label was learned in the coincidental condition. First, the proportion of infant looking to the interesting object in the new phase of the coincidental condition was significantly lower from the recovery and test trials. Indeed, they no longer looked significantly more at the interesting object. Second, the data reflect a trend for a condition effect, such that the overall proportion of looking to the interesting object for the coincidental condition was almost lower than in the conflict condition. Together, these two findings offer support for the claim that infants in the coincidental condition had attached the original label to the target object. They also suggest that these infants noticed the social cues. The only distinguishing feature between the conflict and coincidental conditions is which object the experimenter indicated during the training trial. Thus, even this hint of an effect between the conditions suggests that these children were not completely immune to social cues in the service of word learning.

Dunham et al.'s (1993) findings bear on the present results. They studied whether word learning was facilitated when the experimenter engaged in an "attention-following" versus an "attention-switching" strategy. Prior correlational and experimental results in the literature (e.g., Akhtar, Dunham, & Dunham, 1991; Tomasello & Farrar, 1986) suggested that children whose parents label what their child is already attending to (attention-following), rather than labeling something else (attention-switching), had larger vocabularies. Dunham et al. put these results to a further experimental test, controlling for the variables of motivation and exposure to the novel labels. They found more word learning in the attention-following than in the attention-switching condition, suggesting that word learning works best when it capitalizes on the child's interest.

This is arguably what happened in the coincidental condition, when the object the speaker named was the one the child found most interesting, and the opposite of what happened in the conflict condition. This finding, along with other findings on joint attention (e.g., Tomasello & Farrar, 1986), may help us understand why the 12-month-olds did not show evidence of word learning in the conflict condition. For 12-month-olds, all the cues must be in alignment for word learning to occur. Thus, the data from the conflict condition did not conform to our prediction that the 12-month-olds would attach the novel labels to the most salient objects in the context, regardless of what the speaker labeled.

In discussing why 18-month-olds in their study did not mismap a name to the wrong referent, Dunham et al. (1993) concluded that ". . . infants at this age may be sensitive to the presence of competing cues from the adult" (p. 831). In their study, the competing cues had to do with the child having to decide if the experimenter was labeling her own object or one in the child's possession. In the present experiment, where the children were 6 months younger than the Dunham participants, the competing cues emanated from differential stimulus salience—a fairly blatant cue— and the very subtle cue of social eye gaze. Yet, by failing to learn a name for the interesting (or, for that matter, the boring) object in the conflict condition, children as young as 12 months of age revealed a possible sensitivity to the cue of social eye gaze.

Additional evidence that 12-month-olds are sensitive to the cue of eye gaze comes from a study by Baldwin, Brigitte, and Lenna (1997), as cited in Baldwin and Tomasello (1998). Baldwin et al. (1997) reasoned that babies who look at the speaker's face during labeling episodes may not be looking to gauge the speaker's referential intention, but simply because the speaker was engaged in a "noisy activity." To see if babies were really looking for referential information on the speaker's face, Baldwin et al. created a situation that was ambiguous as to which of two objects was being labeled. In comparison to a condition where only one possible referent was present, 12-month-olds (and 18-month-olds) showed a dramatic increase in gaze-checking of the speaker's face. If 12-month-olds were only looking at the speaker out of interest, there should have been no difference between the referentially clear and the referentially ambiguous situation. This study, in combination with our results in the training trials of Experiments 2 and 3, clearly shows that eye gaze is being noticed by 12-month-olds.

Whether 12-month-olds can use eye gaze in service of word learning however, is another story. That is, there might be a large gap between detecting social cues, which the 12-month-olds *can* do, and using these cues to assist them in mapping words onto referents. Experiments 4–6 were designed to explore this question.

OVERALL DISCUSSION

Experiments 1, 2, and 3 addressed three hypotheses: that children are sensitive to multiple cues in word learning, that the relative weightings of the cues for word learning shift with word learning experience, and that children move from an immature to a mature principle of reference. Evidence was presented in favor of each of these claims. Experiments 1 and 2 presented evidence, in the salience phases, that children of all ages were sensitive to perceptual salience. Indeed, even the 24-month-olds were attracted by perceptual salience, although they did not rely on it in the conflict condition when assigning a word to a referent in the test phase. There also is evidence that children at each age were sensitive to social cues. The 19- and 24-month-olds were able to follow social eye gaze and determine word reference, as evidenced by the condition effect observed in the training and test phases of Experiment 1. Furthermore, the 12-month-olds' sensitivity to social eye gaze in the training phases of Experiments 2 and 3, as well as the trend toward a condition effect in the test phases of Experiment 3, reinforces the claim that they are sensitive to multiple cues in the word learning situation, although they might not make full use of these.

Interestingly, the data also suggest that, at the earliest stages of word learning, the cues not only must be present but also must be in alignment for word learning to occur. The failure of 12-month-olds to show any evidence of word learning in the conflict condition of Experiment 3 suggests that the cue of perceptual salience and the cue of social eye gaze must both "point" to the same object. When they do not, word learning becomes very difficult for these infants, who are unsure of which cues are more reliable in the word learning situation. Similarly, Dunham et al. concluded, "in the presence of competing cues, [infants] may adopt the strategy of simply aborting the encoding process rather than risk the linguistic implications of a mapping error" (p. 831).

Experiments 1 and 2 reveal that at the ages of 12 and 24 months, children weight perceptual and social cues very differently. This differential weighting helps explain the changing character of word learning over time. Taken together, the first three experiments suggest that 12-month-olds rely less on the cue of social eye gaze and relatively more on perceptual salience, whereas 24-month-olds rely more on social cues. This confirms our second hypothesis—the weights these cues are given for word learning shift over developmental time. As Table 2 shows for Experiment 1, perceptual salience is weighted heavily at first, then declines (but does not disappear) by 24 months. The weight given to social eye gaze clearly increases, as evidenced by the significant condition effect (seen in the percentage change row for the 19- and 24-month-olds).

Finally, it can be argued that children at 12 months have but an immature principle of reference, as our third hypothesis presumed, approaching the word learning task in a qualitatively different way than the 19- and 24-month-olds. The latter take the perspective of the speaker into account in linking a name to a referent; the former, while sensitive to conflicting cues, only seem to learn words that correspond to their own perspective.

V. WHAT DOES IT TAKE FOR 12-MONTH-OLDS TO LEARN A WORD?

Elizabeth Hennon, He Len Chung, and Ellie Brown

Chapter 4 offered preliminary evidence in support of the three major hypotheses presented in chapter 2. Infants seemed to use both social and attentional cues for word learning and the weights given to these cues showed evidence of shifting over time. Furthermore, the complexion of word learning appeared to change as children, by 24 months of age, overcame competing cues and relied on the speaker's attentional focus. In contrast, 12-month-olds seemed to learn words best only when they coincided with their own attentional focus. That is, only when the attentional cue of perceptual salience was coupled with the cue of social eye gaze in the coincidental condition of Experiment 3 did the 12-month-olds show any evidence of learning a novel label after five exposures.

Prior work (Butterworth & Grover, 1990; Morales et al., 1998; Scaife & Bruner, 1975) reports that by 12 months of age, infants can follow an experimenter's or their mother's eye gaze to one of several targets. We found evidence of this in the training trials of Experiments 2 and 3. In Experiment 1, however, because 12-month-olds chose to focus disproportionately on the "exciting" toy during test phases, regardless of what was receiving a label during training, their ability to follow eye gaze may have been masked. One possibility is that by designing Experiments 1, 2, and 3 as we did, with a strong countercue in perceptual salience, we inadvertently minimized 12-month-olds' ability to use social eye gaze in the service of word learning. Indeed, research suggests that 12-month-olds can interpret many kinds of social cues. By way of example, Baldwin et al. (1996) demonstrated that even 12-month-olds could use joint visual focus to interpret a speaker's emotional affect. If young infants can engage in social referencing to extract emotional information, then they might be able to use their social sensitivity in the service of word learning.

The experiments presented in this chapter examine the effects of social cues, such as pointing, handling, and eye gaze, in the absence of attentional cues. Thus, these experiments explore what it takes for 12-month-olds to learn a word when salience is removed. Can eye gaze alone lead infants to attach a novel label to a novel object? What about pointing, handling, multiple labels, extra time, or any combination of these cues? Experiments 4 through 9 address these questions and give further evidence that a confluence of cues is necessary for word learning to take place.

The first experiment was designed to investigate whether babies would be able to use eye gaze to learn a novel word when the lure of perceptual salience was removed through the use of objects with equal salience. Therefore, to determine which of the two objects is the referent of the label, infants have only the cue of eye gaze. Note that eye gaze, in our studies, is a complex cue in that it involves a turn of the head, a change of posture, a movement of the eyes, and a change in the direction of the voice from midline. If infants were able to use this kind of "eye gaze" to learn novel words, we would still need further research to discern which component(s) were being used by babies. Nonetheless, if 12-month-olds can use the cue of eye gaze to learn labels for objects of equal salience, it would indicate that eye gaze is a powerful word learning cue even for infants producing their first words. If, however, word learning does not occur in this situation, there are two possible explanations. First, it may be that eye gaze by itself is too subtle a cue for youngsters at this age. Infants may not have learned to use eye gaze and *only* eye gaze to support word learning as our 24-month-olds have revealed. Second, 12-month-olds may be able to use eye gaze but only when it is coupled with additional cues in the coalition. Multiple, overlapping cues may be essential at the start of word learning when babies have but an immature and fragile principle of reference.

EXPERIMENT 4: THE IMPACT OF EYE GAZE ON WORD LEARNING IN THE ABSENCE OF PERCEPTUAL SALIENCE

The purpose of this experiment was to see whether 12-month-olds could utilize the cue of eye gaze to learn words in the Interactive IPLP with objects of roughly equal salience. If we removed the "hook" of perceptual salience, it might be possible to evaluate the impact of the subtle social cue of eye gaze in a situation when it is not competing with other word learning cues.

Method

Participants. Sixteen children (half boys and half girls) composed the final sample. The age range was 11.79 to 13.82 ($M = 12.672$, $SD = 0.542$). A total of six additional participants (22%) were lost due to fussiness and experimenter error.

63

Procedure and stimuli. This experiment utilized the Interactive IPLP and followed the same procedure as Experiment 1, with the exception of stimuli. We used two pairs of equally salient novel objects that were consistently presented in the same pairs. The first pair was a corn butterer and a tea leaf strainer that were similar in size and shape. The other pair consisted of a white garlic press and a green lint remover, also of similar shape and size.

Results

Overall analysis. Table 4 depicts the mean looking times to the equally salient objects at all phases. A repeated-measures three-way (phase: salience/training/test) ANOVA was run. It yielded no significant main effect of phase, $F(2, 30) = 0.136$, $MSE = 0.0026$, $p = .8738$. To complement this analysis, we also applied a one-sample test against the chance level of .50 to each of the phases.

Salience trials. The objects were found to be of equivalent salience. The one-sample analysis against the chance level of .50 was not significant, $t(15) = 0.475$, $p = .6791$.

Training trials. Children also did not watch the target object significantly more than the non-target when it was labeled with social eye gaze, $t(15) = 0.505$, $p = .689$, $d = 0.17$.

Test trials. Children also did not look proportionately more at the targeted object during test trials, $t(15) = 0.01$, $p = .503$, $d = .0025$. Therefore, children did not attach the label using social eye gaze.

Discussion

This experiment demonstrated that in a task utilizing objects of equal salience, 12-month-olds were unable to take advantage of the social cue of eye gaze to attach labels to their correct referents. In this task, infants did not seem to notice such a subtle social cue. That is, they showed no evidence of following eye gaze in either the training or test trials. Thus, when perceptual salience was removed from the coalition of cues, eye gaze was not sufficient, of itself, to direct attention to the target object or to promote word learning.

Previous research has indicated that 11-month-olds can, in fact, reliably follow eye gaze to an object (Corkum & Moore, 1995). So what kept our participants from demonstrating this ability? Significant procedural

TABLE 4

EXPERIMENTS 4–11: MEAN LOOKING TIME (SD) IN SECONDS TO
EQUALLY SALIENT OBJECTS AS A FUNCTION OF PHASE

	Salience	Training	Test
Experiment 4 (Eye Gaze Alone)			
Target	2.34 (0.49)	1.87 (0.87)	1.89 (0.51)
Non-Target	2.40 (0.54)	2.02 (0.76)	1.87 (0.76)
% to Target	49.3	48.0	48.9
Experiment 5 (Touching and Eye Gaze)			
Target	2.61 (1.00)	6.54 (2.40)	2.42 (0.62)
Non-Target	2.65 (0.84)	2.72 (1.85)	2.37 (0.50)
% to Target	49.6	70.6**	50.5
Experiment 6 (Handling and Eye Gaze)			
Target	2.88 (0.75)	6.66 (2.04)	2.00 (0.81)
Non-Target	2.39 (0.68)	1.48 (1.14)	1.93 (0.65)
% to Target	54.6	81.8**	50.8
Experiment 7 (Handling, Eye Gaze, and 10 Labels)			
Target	2.67 (0.57)	11.42 (3.71)	2.74 (0.77)
Non-Target	2.70 (0.77)	3.65 (3.50)	2.14 (0.72)
% to Target	49.7	75.7**	56.1*
Experiment 8 (Eye Gaze and 10 Labels)			
Target	2.72 (0.89)	5.43 (2.44)	2.35 (0.57)
Non-Target	2.60 (0.65)	4.02 (2.94)	2.18 (0.71)
% to Target	51.1	57.4*	51.8
Experiment 9 (Handling, Eye Gaze, and Longer Labeling Time)			
Target	2.54 (0.98)	8.18 (6.19)	2.27 (0.83)
Non-Target	2.50 (0.83)	3.18 (1.56)	1.83 (0.69)
% to Target	50.3	72.0**	55.3*
Experiment 10 (Handling, Eye Gaze, and 10 "Labels"—Mouth Noises)			
Target	2.60 (0.89)	12.25 (4.21)	2.79 (0.69)
Non-Target	2.89 (0.88)	4.66 (2.42)	1.86 (0.59)
% to Target	47.3	72.4**	60.0*
Experiment 11 (Handling, Eye Gaze, and 10 "Labels"—Object Sounds)			
Target	2.44 (0.88)	13.76 (4.54)	2.21 (0.65)
Non-Target	2.49 (0.97)	3.14 (1.89)	2.00 (0.52)
% to Target	49.5	81.4**	52.5

Note.—Planned contrasts against a theoretical chance value of 50% were used, *$p < .05$, **$p < .01$.

differences between past studies and our present investigation may account for our participants' failure to follow the experimenter's gaze to a target. It is possible that the design of our word learning task created a situation that muddied the connection between the eye gaze cue and its intended referent. In both the Corkum and Moore study and our own experiment, infants were presented with two different objects. In the former study, however, objects were placed over 80 in. apart, while objects in our study were separated by just 12 in. The result of this differential spacing was that the experimenter in the Corkum and Moore study was required to rotate her head almost 90° from center, while our experimenter turned her head only 45° in order to look at and label the target object. The fact that the two objects in our study fell into a smaller visual range for the infants may have produced additional ambiguity about what the experimenter was labeling. Furthermore, unlike the Corkum and Moore study, in which the experimenter and infant engaged in a face-to-face interaction, our experimenter was situated behind a display board, with her face on a plane approximately 12 in. above that of the infant.

More important, perhaps, was the context itself. Our task had much more linguistic stimulation than most tasks of infant social sensitivity. The process of directing eye gaze was embedded within a larger social context, one in which language played a critical role. Perhaps the addition of language complicated the task over that of Corkum and Moore (1995).

Although the design of our word learning task may seem demanding in comparison, we believe that it more closely approximates real-world word learning situations. Imagine an adult who is speaking to an infant playing on the floor. Even if the adult were to sit down next the infant on the ground, her face would most likely be at least a foot higher than that of the infant. In addition, because objects in the real world are seldom found in isolation, infants are often challenged, much like in our own task, to determine which of many objects present is the referent of a speaker's eye gaze. While for 24-month-olds, this challenge seems not to be an obstacle to word learning (Experiment 1 and Moore et al., 1999), it may well be a barrier for 12-month-olds when eye gaze is not accompanied by other social or attentional cues.

Nonetheless, regardless of the reason why our youngest participants were unable to follow social eye gaze, it is reasonable to assume that more obvious social cues may be needed to promote successful word-object mappings in the absence of a highly salient object. To assess this possibility, the impact of an additional social cue, touching, was evaluated. In the next experiment, therefore, we added the cue of object touching. If the experimenter did not just look at the object but touched it too, babies would perhaps be able to follow the experimenter to the target object during training. And, if they could follow the experimenter to the target object during training, we would expect that they would show word learning.

EXPERIMENT 5: THE IMPACT OF OBJECT TOUCHING AND EYE GAZE ON WORD LEARNING IN THE ABSENCE OF PERCEPTUAL SALIENCE

This experiment used eye gaze and object touching—in the form of an index finger point—as cues for word learning in the Interactive IPLP. By about 12 months of age, infants can follow a point instead of just looking at the pointing hand the way younger babies do (Butterworth & Grover, 1990). Baldwin and Markman (1989) posit that infants have begun to understand the "pragmatic force" of pointing gestures by the time they first learn words. To increase the likelihood that infants would be able to link the experimenter's cues with the target object, we decided not to just point, but to actually touch the referent with one extended index finger. Unlike eye gaze alone, or even typical pointing, an index finger touch specifies a speaker's referent by creating a physical link between the speaker and the referent. Recognition of such a link would most likely enable infants to participate in this adult-initiated episode of joint attention. Given that successful joint attention is important to word learning, and that it was not achieved in Experiment 4, we predicted that the addition of touching would promote shared attentional focus and facilitate word learning. That is, we anticipated that infants would now follow the experimenter to the target object during the training phase and would possibly learn the object's name.

If the addition of the social cue of touching resulted in successful word learning, it would suggest that eye gaze alone was too subtle a word learning cue to ensure 12-month-old word learning. If, however, 12-month-olds are still unable to take advantage of the coalition of touch and eye gaze, we will have to consider the possibility that in order to learn words, infants this young may need to be exposed to even more cues in combination. For 12-month-olds, social cues, in and of themselves, may not be sufficient to get word learning off the ground.

Method

Participants. Sixteen children (half boys and half girls) composed the final sample. The age range was 11.79 to 13.82 ($M = 12.672$, $SD = 0.542$). A total of four additional participants (20%) were lost due to fussiness and experimenter error.

Procedure and stimuli. The procedure differed from Experiment 4 only by the addition of the social cue of touching. Thus, while offering the label during training, the experimenter reached around the display board from the same side where the target object was located, and without moving the object, touched it with one index finger. The experimenter repeated the label five times while keeping her finger on the object. Throughout training, the experimenter alternated between locking eye gaze with the infant and looking at the target object.

Results

Overall analysis. Again, Table 4 depicts the mean looking times to the equally salient objects at all phases. A repeated-measures three-way (phase: salience/training/test) ANOVA was run. It yielded a significant main effect of phase, $F(2, 30) = 19.081$, $MSE = 0.026$, $p < .0001$. To complement this analysis, we also applied a one-sample test against the chance level of .50 to each of the phases.

Salience trials. Once again, the objects were found to be of equivalent salience. The one-sample analysis against the chance level of .50 was non-significant, $t(15) = 0.206$, $p = .5802$.

Training trials. Children did watch the target object significantly more than the non-target as it was labeled with touching, $t(15) = 6.921$, $p < .0001$, $d = 1.73$. Notice that this effect size for training is quite large.

Test trials. Once again, children did not look proportionately more at the targeted object during test trials, $t(15) = 0.123$, $p = .452$, $d = .03$, even when this object was indicated both by social eye gaze and object touching during training.

Discussion

The purpose of Experiment 5 was to see if babies could learn novel labels with objects of equal salience when the cue of object touching was added to the cue of social eye gaze. Infants' increased attention to the target during training (in comparison to Experiment 4) demonstrates that babies were now able to follow the experimenter to the target object. It may be the case that the interaction of touch and eye gaze successfully erased any ambiguity about the referent of the experimenter's label. Although babies demonstrated sensitivity to the addition of the cue of touch, however, word learning still did not occur. In test trials, participants could not take advantage of the coalition of touch and eye gaze to attach labels to the correct referents. These results suggest the existence of an interesting paradox, a paradox already observed in Experiments 1 and 2: The ability to follow social cues, like pointing and touching, may initially be a separate, decoupled accomplishment from the ability to use these cues to assist word learning.

Apparently, the interaction of touch and eye gaze still did not provide enough word learning information for 12-month-old infants. Given that joint attention to the target object occurred during training, it is a puzzle why word learning still did not occur. Recall that in Experiment 3, word learning apparently occurred in the coincidental condition and object touching was not a cue. In that experiment, perceptual salience seemed to remove ambiguity about which of the two objects was the referent of the novel label. In this experiment, although infants looked longer at the target compared to the non-target during training, it appears that the addition of touch did not remove this referential ambiguity since infants still showed no evidence of having learned the label during the test phase. This suggests that, in the absence of perceptual salience, babies may need yet more cues to attach a novel label to a novel object. On this interpretation, in the next experiment we added yet another social cue, one that we thought would increase shared attentional focus even further. Perhaps an even greater increase in shared attention during training would allow infants to bridge the gap between successful training trials and subsequent test trials. The cue we added this time was object handling. Object handling entails the touching used in the present experiment and adds the dimension of movement, known to be a powerful attention-getter for babies (see Kellman & Arterberry, 1998).

If the interaction of handling and eye gaze elicits robust attention to the target object during training trials and provides evidence of word learning on the test trials, we will have discovered a coalition of social cues powerful enough to promote accurate label-object mappings in the absence of perceptual salience. If, by contrast, word learning is not demonstrated under these circumstances, we will be inclined to look beyond the range of social cues to understand how 12-month-olds establish stable word-object relationships.

EXPERIMENT 6: THE IMPACT OF OBJECT HANDLING AND EYE GAZE ON WORD LEARNING IN THE ABSENCE OF PERCEPTUAL SALIENCE

Whereas the coalition of cues used in Experiment 5 failed to promote word learning, the significant increase in attention, during training, created by the interaction of touch and eye gaze, prompted us to add another, more blatant social cue. Now the experimenter did more than just touch the object with an index finger; she lifted the object and slowly rotated it as she conducted training. We expected that the cue of an experimenter manipulating the object would enhance the attentional value of the target. Prior research (Moore et al., 1999) had already demonstrated that object movement was a salient cue, although in that study the experimenter did not handle the object. Rather, the object appeared to move by itself. When the experimenter's eye gaze was directed at the moving object, children in both age groups had no difficulty learning the novel labels. It was only when movement was put in conflict with eye gaze (the experimenter looked at the static object) that 18-month-olds' word learning broke down. From these results, there was reason to believe that handling the labeled object would: (a) increase 12-month-olds' attention to the target during training relative to Experiment 5; (b) further reduce any ambiguity about the referent of the adult's label; and (c) increase the level of joint attention, which should translate into successful word learning.

Method

Participants. Sixteen children (half boys and half girls) composed the final sample. The age range was 11.49 to 13.89 ($M = 12.717$, $SD = 0.601$). A total of three additional participants (15%) were lost due to fussiness and experimenter error.

Procedure and stimuli. The procedure differed from Experiment 5 only by the addition of object handling. During the training phase, the experimenter offered a novel label while looking at and also handling the target object. The experimenter reached around the display board from the same side where the target object was located, lifted the object approximately 3 in. and slowly rotated it. The object never moved to the midline of the display board. Instead, it remained on its designated side while the non-target remained stationary on the other side in the infant's view. While alternating between locking eye gaze with the infant and looking at the target object, the experimenter constantly rotated the target object and repeated the novel label five times.

Results

Overall analysis. Again, Table 4 depicts the mean looking times to the equally salient objects at all phases. A repeated-measures three-way (phase: salience/training/test) ANOVA was run. It yielded a significant main effect of phase, $F(2, 30) = 32.763$, $MSE = 0.481$, $p < .0001$. To complement this analysis, we also applied a one-sample test against the chance level of .50 to each of the phases.

Salience trials. Once again the objects were found to be of equivalent salience. The one-sample analysis against the chance level of .50 was non-significant, $t(15) = 1.512$, $p = .0757$.

Training trials. Children again watched the targeted object significantly more than the non-target as it was labeled with social eye gaze and handling, $t(15) = 11.234$, $p < .0001$, $d = 2.80$. This effect size for training is very large. Furthermore, even compared to the coincidental condition of Experiment 1 (69.4% to interesting), babies in this experiment watched the target object significantly longer (81.8% to interesting) during training, $t(30) = 2.17$, $p = .03$.

Test trials. Once again, however, children did not look proportionately more at the targeted object during test trials, $t(15) = 0.083$, $p = .4673$, $d = .02$.

Discussion

Although infants devoted greater visual fixation time to the target versus the non-target object during training, they still failed to successfully attach labels to their correct referents. Thus, results from this experiment further emphasize that the ability to *follow* social cues to a referent is separate from the ability to attach a label to that referent. Although the social cues of eye gaze and handling clearly succeeded in directing infants' attention to the target object during training, babies were unable to attach the label to its correct referent. Even when infants allocated over 80% (approximately 6 s) of their attention to the target object during training trials, they could not establish stable links between objects and their labels.

At this stage, it remains difficult to pinpoint what exactly accounts for the discrepancy between a high proportion of shared attention to the target object during training and little evidence of word learning on the subsequent test trials. As we added different social cues from one experiment to the next, we saw significant increases in visual fixation on the target object between the training sessions of the three successive experiments. Percentages of visual fixation times on the target object increased from 48% during the training trials in Experiment 4, to 70.6% in Experiment 5, to 81.8% in Experiment 6. Yet, test trial data from all three experiments are nearly identical. Despite an apparent increase in attention during training in Experiments 4 through 6, there was no evidence of word learning on the test trials.

Because the experimenter was able to control the presentation of the stimuli with precision during training in all three experiments, we were able to separate the infants' ability to follow the experimenter to the target object from their ability to accurately attach the label to its correct referent. Thus, as seen in training in Experiments 5 and 6, children exhibited an awareness of these social cues. It might be thought that they used these social cues to discern which object was receiving the label. That did not seem, however, to be the case. Training performance did not predict word learning. Detection of these cues did not mean that children could use them in service to word learning.

Perhaps object handling done by the experimenter, however, is not as effective as object handling done by the child. If done by the experimenter, object handling falls into the realm of a social cue for word learning. If done by the child, it falls in the category of object exploration. We did, however, consider conducting a further experiment allowing the infants themselves to manipulate the objects during training, until we realized that there would be significant variations in training experiences between participants. From our observations of familiarization trials where infants were allowed to handle each of the novel objects for 26 s, children played with the objects in very different ways. Some engaged in active play, picking up the object and trying to explore its properties, whereas others simply looked at it, not touching it at all. Some infants chose to put the objects in their mouths, an action that increased the breadth of their sensory experience with the object but decreased visual exposure, which is more likely to be needed in making a word-referent hook-up. Aside from the fact that having the experimenter handle the object during training made object handling a social cue, it precluded the inadvertent inclusion of these confounding variables.

We originally hypothesized that the dynamic interaction of the cues of eye gaze and object handling would enable our participants to form correct word-object mappings. Given the failure to achieve positive results, we can conclude that the coalition of these social cues does not lead to successful word learning. After using three social cues of increasing "strength" and five repetitions of a novel label, we are forced to conclude that social cues, in and of themselves, may not be enough to facilitate early word learning.

OVERALL DISCUSSION OF EXPERIMENTS 4–6

In Experiments 1, 2, and 3 we discovered that infants demonstrate differential abilities in taking advantage of eye gaze in the service of word learning. Twelve-month-olds in some experiments (the training phases of Experiments 2 and 3) showed some *sensitivity* to eye gaze, but only 19- and 24-month-olds could make use of eye gaze in establishing a reliable word-to-world mapping. In addition, when we removed the "hook" of perceptual salience from Experiments 4, 5, and 6 of this chapter, we were able to reveal that other social cues are differentially effective in eliciting *attention* in a labeling situation. But their effectiveness in eliciting infants' attention toward an object during training did not seem to be related to word learning. We can conclude that infants' ability to establish joint attention is initially separate from their ability to extract the information necessary to attach words to their referents.

It is widely accepted that episodes of joint attention are important to word learning, but given the results of Experiments 4, 5, and 6, we must consider why, for our 12-month-olds, such episodes stopped short of generating evidence for word-object mappings. Perhaps these infants resisted attaching a label to an object hastily (after exposure to only five labels) since they were not certain about the purpose of the word learning task. Without the presence of an obvious, highly salient object, infants may not have been sufficiently motivated to attach a label after so few exposures to it. Being conservative is an adaptive strategy at 12 months of age before the child is clear about (a) the cues that feed into word learning and (b) what weights to assign them. As Baldwin (1991) has pointed out, 30–50% of parental labels do not name the thing that the child is attending to at the moment. If 12-month-olds readily attached labels after but a few exposures, they would have a great deal of *unlearning* to do.

Because we know that labels *are* learned, however, we are still intrigued to understand what might make this happen in the absence of differential perceptual salience. Indeed, Woodward et al. (1994) reported that 13-month-old children are capable of learning that a novel word refers to a novel object. In their study, an experimenter followed the child's line of regard and waited until the child began to play with the target object before labeling it. Then the experimenter labeled the object three times. The child was then given a different toy to play with, and the labeling ceased until the next time the child became interested in the target. Training then continued, until the novel object was labeled nine times. In this situation, children were able to learn that the new word referred to the new object.

Why do children learn the new word in the Woodward et al. (1994) study but not in the studies presented above? Two possible reasons are the differences in task demands and in the age of the participants. The mean age of the Woodward et al. sample was 13.6 months, whereas the mean age of the children in Experiments 1 through 6 was 12.58. Although small differences in age at young ages are often important, it is not clear whether this difference—by itself—is responsible for the different findings. Next, we examine the task demands of Woodward et al.'s (1994) study as compared to the present experiments.

One major difference between Woodward et al. (1994) and the present studies is that they labeled the target a total of nine times, while we only provided five presentations of the novel word. Perhaps children at the start of word learning need to hear novel words more often than they will later on. Yet, the fact that 12-month-old children in the coincidental condition of Experiment 3 may have learned a novel word with but five exposures indicates that frequency of exposure cannot be the whole story. A crucial difference may be that in Woodward et al.'s study the *child's* interest determined when the experimenter provided the label. Only when the infant's focus was on the target toy did the experimenter begin to label the object. Furthermore, Woodward et al. removed the non-target toy at just the moment when the child focused on the target object so that there was no question about which toy was being labeled. In sharp contrast, we attempted to *direct* the child's focus of attention onto a target object of the experimenter's choosing and to label that object in the presence of a non-target object.

Previous studies suggested that an 18-month-old child would learn novel words more readily when the adult labels an object within the *child's* focus of attention rather than an object in the adult's focus of attention. In this way, the child does not have to follow the adult's line of regard (Dunham et al., 1993; Tomasello & Farrar, 1986). Perhaps the coincidental condition of Experiment 3 created an "attention-following" (Dunham et al., 1993) situation, the very context known to promote word learning. By our having the experimenter label the more interesting object, the child could then focus on the label per se. In that case, the child did not have to work at determining the adult's focus of attention (an "attention-switching" situation; Dunham et al., 1993). Rather in an attention-following task, all the child's effort can be spent on learning that the new word refers to the novel object. Based on infants' difficulties with the conflict condition in Experiment 3, we attempted to simplify the task by equating the salience of the objects in chapter 5.

Instead, we may have inadvertently *increased* task difficulty by requiring the child first to determine which object was the target, and, second, to focus on the new name. Ironically, then, Experiments 4, 5, and 6 may have made the word learning task harder rather than easier for children. This added demand of following the adult's lead may have interfered with infants' word learning.

The question becomes under what circumstances can a 12-month-old learn a new word in an equal salience task. That is, when one object is no more attractive and attention-getting than the other object is, what does it take for a baby to find a target object and to attach a label to that object? One clue might lie in Woodward et al.'s (1994) study. Perhaps, in the absence of the cue of perceptual salience, hearing the label a greater number of times may help the child. Five presentations of a label might not be enough.

EXPERIMENT 7: WORD LEARNING OCCURS IN 12-MONTH-OLDS WITH MULTIPLE SOCIAL CUES AND 10 REPETITIONS OF A NOVEL NAME

The purpose of this experiment was to see whether, in the absence of the cue of perceptual salience, 12-month-olds could learn a novel word with an increased number of exposures to the new label. Based on Woodward et al. (1994), the number of repetitions of the new word was increased from 5 to 10, one more than Woodward et al. had used. As the only difference between the present study and Experiment 6 was in the number of times the new word was spoken during the labeling phase, the results from this study can be directly compared with those in Experiment 6. This study was affectionately referred to as the "bludgeoning" study as we were metaphorically "hitting the children over the head" with the novel label and with multiple social cues.

Method

Participants. Thirty-two children (half boys and half girls) composed the final sample. The age range was 11.76 to 13.43 ($M = 12.59$, $SD = 0.427$). A total of 13 additional participants (28%) were lost due to fussiness and experimenter error.

Procedure and stimuli. Using the Interactive IPLP, pairs of novel objects balanced for attractiveness were presented. These were the same objects as those used in Experiments 4–6. The critical difference between this study and those experiments, however, was in the labeling phase. The experimenter placed both novel objects on the table in front of the display board. Once the experimenter attracted the child's attention, the experimenter picked up one of the objects (the target), looked down at it, and rotated it slowly while beginning to label it. After labeling the object two times, the experimenter regained the child's attention. Once the child was again looking at the experimenter, the experimenter looked back at the target object, and rotated it while labeling it three times. Thus far, the procedure is identical to that of Experiment 6. After the fifth label, however, the sequence was repeated in its entirety. Thus, the training phase progressed as follows: "Johnny, look at the *modi*, the *modi*. Hey! Johnny, look at the *modi*. It's a *modi*, a *modi*! Johnny, look at the *modi*, the *modi*. Hey! Johnny, look at the *modi*. This is a *modi*, a *modi*."

Following this training phase, the novel objects were removed from the table, and were velcroed onto the Fagan board. The test trials were conducted in a manner identical to those in Experiment 6.

Results

Overall analysis. Again, Table 4 depicts the mean looking times to the equally salient objects at all phases. A repeated-measures three-way (phase: salience/training/test) ANOVA was run. It yielded a significant main effect of phase, $F(2, 62) = 47.33$, $MSE = 0.681$, $p < .0001$. To complement this analysis, we also applied a one-sample test against the chance level of .50 to each of the phases.

Salience trials. Once again the objects were found to be of equivalent salience. The one-sample analysis against the chance level of .50 was non-significant, $t(31) = 0.12$, $p = .9054$.

Training trials. Children again watched the target object significantly more than the non-target as it was labeled 10 times with handling, $t(31) = 11.856$, $p < .0001$, $d = 2.09$. Notice that this effect size for training is extremely large.

Test trials. In this experiment, unlike in the previous three, however, children *did* look proportionately more at the targeted object during test trials, $t(31) = 2.674$, $p = .0119$, $d = .47$, a large effect size. Therefore, children did attach the label when the targeted object was signified by handling and labeled 10 times.

Discussion

The purpose of Experiment 7 was to see whether 12-month-olds could learn novel labels for equally salient objects in a task that presented novel objects in contexts with multiple social cues and 10 exposures to the label during the training phase. During the training phase, children did indeed look longer at the target than the non-target objects. The children in Experiment 6 also looked longer at the target during training, however, but failed to show word learning. Thus, increased looking time at the target during training is not sufficient to enable word learning. Once the child is focused on the correct toy, the adult must then provide enough information for the child to learn that the new word refers to the new object. In Experiment 6, it seemed that five labels were not enough for the children to learn the new word in the absence of the cue of differential perceptual salience. In Experiment 7, however, 10 labels proved to be sufficient. By increasing the number of presentations of the novel label, this experiment demonstrated that 12-month-old infants could learn that a new word refers to a target object. One-year-old children do not need the target object to be inherently more perceptually salient than the non-target object. But, in the absence of the powerful cue of perceptual salience, and in the presence of more than one potential referent, the label apparently must be provided more frequently.

Perhaps *all* that is needed for word learning to occur in the 12-month-old is a certain number of labels that exceed some threshold of exposure combined with eye gaze. If that is true, then children should learn novel labels in a situation where 10 repetitions are offered accompanied by eye gaze that singles out the target object. Perhaps the multiple social cues made available to them in this experiment are unnecessary if they can hear 10 repetitions of the label. The next experiment evaluates this alternative by presenting 12-month-olds with equal salience objects, only the social cue of eye gaze, and 10 labels. If children can learn words in that experiment it would suggest that the emergentist coalition model is incorrect. Emphasis on the necessity for multiple, overlapping cues for word learning must be either wrong or overstated. If children do not show evidence of word learning in the next experiment, however, it will confirm the requirement of a coalition of overlapping cues to support word learning in novices.

EXPERIMENT 8: WORD LEARNING IN 12-MONTH-OLDS IS NOT SUPPORTED BY EYE GAZE AND 10 REPETITIONS OF THE NOVEL LABEL

The prior experiment virtually bludgeoned children with word learning information and children did indeed learn novel words. The purpose of this experiment is to see whether that result was simply the result of providing 10 labels and eye gaze. Perhaps the rest of the social cues offered are unnecessary if the label is heard many times. To test this hypothesis, we repeated Experiment 4 with the change that we now offered the label 10 times instead of 5. Therefore, the same, equally salient objects and the same procedure were used. (Note that this procedure was also the same as that of Experiment 7, except handling was removed.)

Method

Participants. Sixteen children (half boys and half girls) composed the final sample. The age range was 12.16 to 13.43 ($M = 12.839$, $SD = 0.365$). A total of six additional subjects (16%) were lost due to fussiness and experimenter error.

Procedure and stimuli. This experiment followed the same procedure and used the same two pairs of equally salient novel objects as Experiment 4. Ten labels were used, however, instead of five. That is, infants saw a novel object indicated using social eye gaze, and heard the experimenter label that object 10 times, in the form, "Look, it's a *modi*, a *modi*. See the *modi*?"

Results

Overall analysis. Again, Table 4 depicts the mean looking times to the equally salient objects at all phases. A repeated-measures three-way (phase: salience/training/test) ANOVA was run. It yielded a significant main effect of phase, $F(2, 30) = 3.907$, $MSE = 0.038$, $p = .0310$. To complement this analysis, we also applied a one-sample test against the chance level of .50 to each of the phases.

Salience trials. Once again the objects were found to be of equivalent salience. The one-sample analysis against the chance level of .50 was non-significant, $t(15) = 0.142$, $p = .888$.

Training trials. Children in this experiment did watch the target object significantly more than the non-target as it was labeled with social eye gaze, $t(15) = 2.617$, $p = .0194$, $d = .654$. This effect size for training is moderate.

Test trials. Children, however, did *not* look proportionately more at the targeted object during test trials, $t(15) = 1.101$, $p = .2882$, $d = .275$. Therefore, children did not attach the label using social eye gaze when a label was provided 10 times. Furthermore, given the effect size, this result would need prohibitively large power in order to be shown significant.

Discussion

When we found in Experiment 7 that 10 labels enabled babies to learn the names of equally salient objects, an immediate test of the emergentist coalition model of word learning presented itself. Would babies show us that if they heard 10 repetitions of the target label, they could now learn novel words with just the minimal social cue of eye gaze? There was reason to believe that this might be the case, given that Experiments 2 and 3 had provided some evidence that 12-month-olds were indeed sensitive to eye gaze. Perhaps unequal object salience in earlier experiments masked their ability to use this cue. In fact, this was the rationale for Experiment 4. When Experiment 4 did not show word learning, we kept adding social cues in Experiments 5 and 6, still to no avail. Once we changed to more repetitions of the labels, however, in Experiment 7, learning was now seen. It was reasonable, therefore, to conjecture that Experiment 4 (and 5 and 6, for that matter) might also have worked if we had used 10 labels.

The failure of children to learn words in the present experiment confirms the complexity of the process for young children. In comparison to Experiment 7, which offered the labels 10 times in combination with multiple, overlapping social cues, Experiment 8 only offered eye gaze and 10 labels. This latter combination of cues in the coalition was not sufficient to promote word learning. Indeed, it appears that this experiment has supported the view that for the youngest learners, cues must be "piled up" on the referent or word learning will not occur.

Given that Experiment 8 did not work, we next ask exactly what aspect of the training phase in Experiment 7 was responsible for the word learning effect in that experiment. Not only was the label repeated more often during the training phase, but it also took more *time* to say the target word 10 times rather than five times. (The mean training time was 26.53 seconds as compared to 12.58 seconds for Experiment 6.) The difference between the outcome of Experiments 6 and 7, therefore, might be the increase in the *duration* of the training phase rather than in the number of repetitions of the new word per se. Experiment 9 was designed to determine whether the frequency of the label or the amount of time spent in the training phase was the critical factor in 12-month-olds' ability to learn the novel words.

EXPERIMENT 9: MORE TIME ON TASK ENABLES 12-MONTH-OLDS TO LEARN A NOVEL WORD

Experiment 9 attempted to tease apart the factors potentially contributing to the results from Experiment 7. We know from Experiment 8 that the frequency of the label per se is not responsible for the effect. Perhaps, though, it is the frequency of the label combined with multiple social cues that caused the word learning effect. Either the results were due to exposing children to the label 10 times instead of five (as in Experiment 6), or the results were due to allowing children more time to process the new label. On the former "frequency + social cues explanation," children may need to hear a label a minimum number of times when neither object is highly salient and in the presence of multiple, overlapping social cues. The alternative possibility can be called the "processing explanation." Perhaps 12-month-olds simply need more time (for a variety of possible reasons) in the word learning situation to store the novel labels. To distinguish between these explanations, Experiment 9 presented the target word only five times, as in Experiment 6. The five labels, however, were delivered over the same amount of time as it took to say all 10 repetitions in Experiment 7. This was done by presenting the child with 10 sentences, thereby equalizing the time of presentation with Experiment 7. Yet, within the 10 sentences, the label would only be supplied a total of five times. For example, if in Experiment 7, the child had heard, "Look at the modi. It is a modi," then in Experiment 9 the child heard, "Look at *this*. It is a modi." In this manner, the language stimulation was kept constant, while the number of times the label was offered was cut in half.

If the frequency explanation holds, then the results of Experiment 9 would not be significant. Children should not learn the word with only five presentations of the new label. If the processing explanation bears out, children should learn the novel words as well in this experiment as they did in Experiment 7.

Method

Participants. Twenty-two children (half boys and half girls) composed the final sample. The age range was 11.36 to 13.62 ($M = 12.46$, $SD = .609$). A total of eight additional participants (26%) were lost due to fussiness and experimenter error.

Procedure. Experiment 9 differed from Experiment 7 only in what was said during the training phase. The experimenter labeled the object a total of five times in 10 sentences. The sentences alternated between ending in the new word (i.e., "modi") and in "this" or "this one." Thus, five sentences ended in "modi" and five sentences ended in "this" or "this one." While labeling the object, the experimenter once again stopped periodically to refocus the child's attention, thereby breaking the 10 sentences up into groups of two and three. Thus, training would progress as follows: "Johnny, look at the *modi*. Look at this one. Hey Johnny, look at the *modi*. See this one? It's a *modi*! Johnny, look at the *modi*. Look at this. Johnny, hey Johnny, look at the *modi*. Look at this. It's a *modi*." The test trials used the same procedure as that followed during Experiment 7.

Results

Overall analysis. Again, Table 4 depicts the mean looking times to the equally salient objects at all phases. A repeated-measures three-way (phase: salience/training/test) ANOVA was run. It yielded a significant main effect of phase, $F(2, 42) = 35.382$, $MSE = 0.56$, $p < .0001$. To complement this analysis, we also applied a one-sample test against the chance level of .50 to each of the phases.

Salience trials. Once again the objects were found to be of equivalent salience. The one-sample analysis against the chance level of .50 was non-significant, $t(21) = 0.08$, $p = .531$.

Training trials. As in Experiment 7, children in this experiment did watch the target object significantly more than the non-target as it was labeled with social eye gaze, $t(21) = 15.194$, $p < .0001$, $d = 3.24$, a very large effect size.

Test trials. Children, again as in Experiment 7, looked proportionately more at the targeted object during test trials, $t(21) = 1.804$, $p = .0428$, $d = 0.38$. Therefore, children attached the label when a label was provided five times over 10 sentences accompanied by the social cue of eye gaze and handling.

Discussion

The purpose of Experiment 9 was to distinguish between a frequency explanation and a process explanation for the significant word learning results found in Experiment 7. In Experiment 7, children heard the novel label 10 times instead of 5 times as in Experiment 6. In Experiments 4 through 9, children's visual fixation time during the salience trials indicated that the objects selected were indeed of equivalent attraction to 12-month-olds. Therefore, any differences between the outcomes of these three experiments cannot be attributed to differential object salience. Training was apparently effective in Experiments 5 through 9 since children looked longer at the target object than at the non-target. At this point however, the experiments diverge. Although training *appeared* to be effective in all five experiments, children only showed reliable word learning in Experiments 7 and 9. Thus, both frequency and processing time are necessary but not sufficient in promoting word learning.

Taken together, Experiments 7, 8, and 9 fail to support the frequency explanation. If the sheer number of labels was the critical determinant of word learning, then the results of both Experiments 7 and 8 should have been significant. Instead, these experiments provide partial support for the hypothesis that the *amount of time* spent labeling affects word learning. When 12-month-olds were presented with the difficult task of both determining which object was being labeled *and* learning the label for that object, they required that the adult supply them with much information and support. It was not enough to label the object a mere five times (Experiment 6). It also was not necessary to repeat the word over and over again, as seen in Experiment 8. What these studies suggest is that the infant at the beginning of word learning requires a blend of several different kinds of word learning cues. Indeed, word learning appears to be quite fragile and although possible, occurs only if the environment supports the infant in just the right ways.

OVERALL DISCUSSION

Experiments 7 and 9 demonstrate that 12-month-olds *can* learn a label for a novel object under certain circumstances. Although it is not necessary for an adult to provide endless repetitions of the new word, an adult must do more than simply trust the child to read the adult's mind. When confronted with two novel objects and one novel label, the infant must first determine *which* object is being labeled. In situations where neither object is more perceptually salient, this appears to be a complex task. Researchers such as Dunham and Tomasello have found that infants learn more words when adults follow the *infant's* focus of interest rather than trying to get the infant to follow their focus of attention (Dunham et al., 1993; Tomasello & Farrar, 1986).

Clearly a prerequisite to learning a new word is figuring out which object is being labeled. By 18 or 19 months children will be quite good at making this inference in tasks where it is not very obvious. For example, they will not be fooled into forming an incorrect mapping when they hear a woman behind a screen loudly uttering a label just as they look at a novel object (Baldwin et al., 1996). And they will select the correct object to be the referent of a new label even though the experimenter selects several non-target objects first by mistake (Tomasello & Barton, 1994). But at 12 months, taking the perspective of the speaker and discerning which object is being labeled is not a simple task.

Experiment 7 shows that even at 12 months, one way infants can overcome the hurdle of figuring out which object is being labeled is by hearing the label 10 times at the same time that the adult also provides multiple social cues. Although the two toys presented were equally salient, the infants were able to learn the new word. Experiment 8 suggests that word learning in Experiment 7 was not based exclusively on the social cue of eye gaze or repetitive labeling but, once again, on a confluence of cues, most notably the cue of handling. Experiment 9 suggests that the word learning in Experiment 7 was not based exclusively on the number of repetitions. When five labels were given in a longer amount of time in Experiment 9, infants were also successful in learning new words. The reasons that the manipulation in Experiment 9 was successful are still not clear. Was it the duration of the training phase that made the difference or was it the amount of language spoken during labeling, or were both important? If young infants simply need more time to process information, then the extended duration of the training phase may have done the trick. The increased number of presentations of the label (Experiment 7) or the increased number of sentences during training with only five labels (Experiment 9) may have given the 12-month-olds the time they needed to encode and store the new labels.

A second option is that the increased amount of time in both Experiments 7 and 9 has an indirect effect and does not affect the encoding and storage of the labels per se. At the beginning of the labeling phase, the children necessarily focus on determining which object is being labeled. Only after this problem is solved can the children attend to the spoken labels. More time may allow the child to solve the first task and still have time to learn the new words. It would be interesting to directly test whether more language or more time was responsible for the finding in Experiment 9. That is, even in Experiment 9 the children heard 10 sentences but only half were delivering a label. Perhaps one could perform an experiment in which the five labeling sentences were stretched out to fill time originally taken to deliver 10 sentences. Would that disambiguate these results? Unfortunately, elongating the five sentences across the longer training period created a very unnatural learning context that could not be successfully administered with 1-year-olds. The alternative of saying five sentences normally within the longer period of time sounded equally unnatural. Thus, both experiments were discontinued after running very few, unhappy children. One explanation for the results of Experiments 7 and 9 that does not seem very likely, however, is that this learning was due to an increase in the salience of the target object as a result of the extra attention given to that object during labeling. That is, if salience alone was important, increases in attention during labeling, such as those observed in Experiments 5 and 6, should also have produced evidence of learning. They did not. Thus, while Experiment 5, 6, 7, 8, and 9 all led children to look at the labeled object during *training* trials, only Experiments 7 and 9 led to evidence of word learning in the *test* trials. In this manner, children's attention during labeling is not a good indicator of subsequent performance in test trials. This is a critical point. Referential *sensitivity* during labeling is not the same thing as referential *understanding*.

In sum, early word learning seems to start out as a fragile process that is dependent on the convergence of many factors. Children do not seem to make many inferences (Experiments 4–6) about which object is the referent of the label. Even in an attention-following task, they require multiple, overlapping cues to guide them through the word learning process. In the more difficult attention-switching task, these infants are at a real disadvantage and seem to require not only overlapping cues, but also increased processing time to yoke a word to its referent. Nineteen- and

24-month-old children are much better at reading the social cues and intentions of the speaker and not needing as many cues in the coalition. These older children have gone so far that they can deal with situations in which the referent is far more ambiguous, as when multiple potential referents are revealed. The 12-month-olds have thus demonstrated that they learn words in ways that are qualitatively different than their older counterparts. In the next chapter, we present a series of experiments that investigate the nature of this difference.

VI. IS 12-MONTH-OLD WORD LEARNING DOMAIN-GENERAL, SOCIALLY DETERMINED, OR EMERGENT?

Word learning in 12-month-olds is tenuous, at best. Indeed, we only found clear evidence for word learning when these infants were metaphorically "bludgeoned" with information. These children needed more repetitions of the label (Experiment 7), or more time on task (Experiment 9), and a host of social cues, handling in particular, to learn the novel words (both experiments). In short, 12-month-olds do not seem to learn new words very efficiently. Instead, they seem to require a tremendous amount of converging evidence.

One explanation of our results might lead to the view that an overlapping, emergent process is at work, a process in which cues compete for control. For example, one reason that label-specific effects were not observed in the conflict condition of Experiment 3 might be the very nature of this condition. That is, that one cue (eye gaze) indicated one object (the boring object), while another cue (perceptual salience) indicated the other, interesting object. The resulting competition between these cues may have blocked any strong acquisition. It is only later in development that a cue, such as social eye gaze, becomes sufficient, in and of itself, for word learning. Perhaps successful early lexical acquisition is the emergent result of having more cues in favor of a particular mapping than those cues that do not favor that mapping.

A related explanation suggests that the earliest word learning might be accomplished through reliance on domain-general mechanisms of association. Smith (1999) noted that sensitivity to correlation is one of the most widespread traits in mammalian nervous systems and that it is reasonable to suppose that it plays an important role in word learning. Recently, research by Plunkett and Marchman (1991) and also by Woodward et al. (1994) echoed this associative hypothesis for first word learning. Woodward et al. (1994), however, noted one consequence of this hypothesis. They wrote,

> If words are learned by young babies as nonlinguistic associates, then a *mere contingency between some sound patterns and the presence of some object* [italics added] would be sufficient to produce a learned association. (p. 564)

In other words, if early word learning relies primarily on associative processes, then babies should link, for example, musical notes or noises to objects just as they link words to objects. This question has become the subject of several recent studies concerned with whether, and when, words begin to function differently than other auditory stimuli. These studies, however, reported conflicting results. Some studies have found that 9-month-old infants treat words and tones differently. For example, Balaban and Waxman (1997) found that words and filtered words, but not sine wave tones, caused 9-month-old infants to form a new category. In this study, infants were habituated to slides of different rabbits paired with a tone, a word, or a filtered word. They were then presented with a forced choice display depicting another rabbit and a pig. Infants who heard a word or a filtered word looked longer at the out-of-category slide (the pig) indicating that they had formed a category. Infants in the tone condition, however, preferred to look at another exemplar of the same category (the rabbit) suggesting that they had not formed a category. Xu (1998) conducted a similar study that reported that infants do not treat words and tones alike. Xu presented 9-month-old infants with two occluded toys that appeared sequentially from either side of a screen. In a familiarization phase, the two toys were either labeled with two different words ("ball," "duck") when they appeared, with one word ("toy"), or with two tones whose onset coincided with the objects' appearance. In the following test phase, the occluding screen was removed to reveal either one object (the inconsistent condition) or two objects (the consistent condition). The results suggest that in the two-word condition (but not the one-word condition) infants looked longer at the inconsistent stimulus. That is, they expected to see two objects if they heard two words. They did not look longer at the inconsistent display when they heard two tones, however, again suggesting that infants as young as 9 months of age treat tones differently than they treat words. In both of these experiments, we see evidence that words, but not tones, heighten attention to objects and to object categories. These findings suggest that babies—even in the 1st year of life—may well recognize that language, and not other nonlinguistic stimuli, has special properties.

Other research with children between the ages of 12 and 18 months found the opposite result: Babies apparently use words, gestures, and sounds interchangeably to map onto objects. By way of example, Woodward and Hoyne (1999) reported that 12-month-old infants will accept a whistle sound as a label for an object in a word learning task. In addition, Namy and Waxman (1998) found that 18-month-olds associate both words and gestures with objects. Finally, Namy (1998) found that 17-month-olds treat melodies, gestures, and visual pictograms as labels for objects. In this experiment, children were asked to "look at the _____" (a target picture) and "find another _____," from among three choices, one of which was in the same category. Children performed above chance with melodies, gestures, and pictograms and at chance in a no-label control condition.

To make matters more complicated, another shift was observed in the data between 20 and 26 months of age when nonlinguistic stimuli previously accepted as labels were now rejected. Woodward and Hoyne (1999) reported that babies at 20 months will not accept a whistle any longer as a label and Namy and Waxman (1998) found that at 26 months, children will no longer readily accept gestures as labels. Thus, the research is mixed on whether the domain-general hypothesis is the best characterization for early word learning. On the one hand, studies using words and tones as stimuli often found that words, but not tones, facilitate object categorization and object representation in the last quarter of the 1st year of life (Balaban & Waxman, 1997; Xu, 1998). These domain-specific findings contradict a domain-general associative hypothesis. If word learning is purely unbiased at the beginning, tones might be expected to work to the same degree in these tasks as words. On the other hand, studies that use social interactional paradigms in which the experimenter sets up joint attention with the baby on some object or picture often report different results. Sounds, gestures, and even visual pictograms *are* used as word substitutes. It is a challenge to explain the discrepancies in these findings.

One possibility for the early findings with 9-month-olds is that the tone stimulus is too bizarre for babies. Perhaps tones are so outside babies' experience that they disrupt the babies' processing of the events in these experiments. If this were true, it still leaves us with the problem of why all sorts of nonlinguistic stimuli do seem to function as "labels" until about 20 months of age. For that matter, one is also left with the question of how it is that some symbols (such as those used in sign language and writing) can be first rejected and later accepted as labels for objects in the world. Woodward (1999) attempted reconciliation between the findings showing that young children are willing to accept more stimuli as "labels" than older children are. She suggested that, although all infants (9 months of age) can distinguish between words and tones, once infants recognize that they are in a word learning situation (not until about 12 months of age), communicative intent is weighted more heavily than the particular "label" used. That is, if the social situation signals that an adult is trying to teach a child a label for an object, 12-month-old babies will be happy to comply. They are willing to associate *any* potential label with an object. Their older counterparts, however, have narrowed down the candidate hypotheses about what can serve as a label and reject the wide range of sounds that can be associates to objects in favor of words alone (although presumably visual signs and symbols are still acceptable).

This explanation is tempting. It turns on the assumption that infants—even 12-month-olds—are capable of distinguishing labeling from nonlabeling situations. Prior research conducted by Waxman and Markow (1995), Baldwin et al. (1997), as well by Woodward (1999) suggests that young children may well be able to distinguish between circumstances in which a label is being offered and where it is not. For example, Baldwin et al. (1997) reported that 12-month-olds can tell the difference between a situation where the referent for a label is ambiguous (more than one possible referent) and a situation where it is unambiguous (only a single possible referent). This explanation may not hold, however, given the findings in this *Monograph* that suggest that young infants can be aware of the social cues that indicate that a labeling situation is in progress and still be unable to recruit those cues in that situation for word learning. Furthermore, there is a simpler explanation. The "label" learning in the experiments considered by Woodward (1999) strongly resembles the coincidental condition of Experiment 3, in that only a single, salient object is presented and all cues indicate exactly what is being labeled. A purely social explanation may thus be premature. These infants also had the cue of perceptual salience on their side. For 12-month-olds, with fragile word learning abilities, these experiments, in effect, created an attention-following situation (Dunham et al., 1993). This "emergentist" interpretation of the accounts suggests that infants will override their domain-specific knowledge of the properties of language when faced with a confluence of attentional and social cues. The question remains, however, if the cues for word learning are not in alignment and the word learning task is harder (as in our equal salience experiments), would young infants still look as competent in reading the social situation and attach any potential label to an object?

In this chapter, we explore these three accounts. Are infants willing to accept anything as a label—consistent with domain-general associative accounts? Do they instead only accept socially indicated sounds—consistent with Woodward's hypothesis? Or do they simply bow to an overwhelming number of cues—as is predicted by the emergentist model? We present three experiments to explore these questions. The first two examine whether nonlinguistic noises are mapped onto objects at all. When we found (in Experiment 11) that words are treated differently (which contradicts the equipotential notions of domain-general associative learning), we then examined whether 12-month-olds use communicative support to override these distinctions, as Woodward (1999) suggests, or whether they appear to use multiple overlapping cues, as the coalition model suggests.

Specifically, in Experiment 10, children were presented with mouth noises (in particular, clicks produced with the tongue and the "psst" sound, typically used to get someone's attention) paired with equally salient objects as if they were words. In Experiment 11, we did the same thing, again with equally salient objects, but used digitized sounds as labels. Thus, the major question motivating these two experiments was whether words are privileged associates of objects or whether any auditory stimulus can work equally well in a situation that only involves social cues and does not involve the cue of perceptual salience. In the final experiment of this chapter, we demonstrate that only by adding the attentional cue of perceptual salience do 12-month-old infants use a sound as a label. Thus, we will argue that the best explanation for 12-month-olds' nonlinguistic "word" learning is one that emphasizes the influence of multiple cues, and particularly attentional cues. A social explanation that emphasizes infants' sensitivity to the fact that they are in a labeling situation is insufficient.

EXPERIMENT 10: MOUTH SOUNDS FUNCTION AS LABELS FOR 12-MONTH-OLDS

To explore the domain-general associative hypothesis, we need to examine whether infants will attempt to attach labels of any sort, mouth sounds or digitized noises, to objects in a word learning situation. If this hypothesis is correct, young children should attach both these kinds of sounds to objects in a word learning task, despite the likelihood that they could distinguish between these stimuli and the actual sounds of language. As in Experiment 7, 10 labels were presented since we knew that 12-month-olds could learn novel words under these conditions, even when the cue of differential perceptual salience was removed. Furthermore, in accord with a domain-general associative version of early word learning, mouth sounds like clicks and "pssts" embedded in labeling frames were hypothesized to work as well as words did in Experiment 7.

Method

Participants. Sixteen children (half boys and half girls) composed the final sample. The age range was 12.23 to 13.23 ($M = 12.69$, $SD = 0.287$). A total of eight additional participants (33%) were lost due to fussiness and experimenter error.

Procedure and stimuli. The objects were the same as used in the equal salience experiments. The procedure was also identical to Experiment 7 in chapter 6. However, mouth sounds were substituted in place of the labels for the two trial blocks of training trials and test trials. The two mouth sounds used were a click produced by the tongue at the side of the mouth and the "psst" sound used to get someone's attention. For example, in the test trials a baby heard, "Look at the [click, click]! See the [click, click]?" As in Experiment 7, the experimenter "labeled" the target ten times and handled the object during the training trials.

Results

Overall analysis. Table 4 depicts the mean looking times to the equally salient objects at all phases. A repeated-measures three-way (phase: salience/ training/test) ANOVA was run. It yielded a significant main effect of phase, $F(2,30) = 30.055$, $MSE = .274$, $p < .0001$. To complement this analysis, we applied a one-sample test against the chance level of .50 to each of the phases.

Salience trials. Once again the objects were found to be of equivalent salience. The one-sample analysis against the chance level of .50 was not significant, $t(15) = 1.219$, $p = .879$.

Training trials. Children watched the target object significantly more than the non-target as it was labeled with the mouth noises, $t(15) = 6.255$, $p < .0001$, $d = 1.56$.

Test trials. Children also looked at the targeted object during test trials, $t(15) = 4.073$, $p = .0005$, $d = 1.01$. Therefore, children attached the mouth noises to the objects, apparently treating them on a par with words in this respect. These effect sizes are comparable to those found in Experiment 7 with words.

Discussion

To examine whether any auditory stimulus would be an equally effective label for a novel object, this experiment attempted to teach 12-month-olds mouth noises presented in labeling frames. That is, the mouth noises were offered to babies, just as real words would be, embedded in sentences that are used to name objects. Equally salient objects were used in the same procedure as that used in Experiment 7, with the experimenter's eye gaze focused on the target as she handled the target object and offered 10 "labels."

Training proved to be as effective as in Experiment 7 in drawing children's attention to the target, a finding that is, in itself, informative. It suggests that hearing mouth noises did not disrupt children's attention to the target object. Children did not seem to distinguish between words and mouth noises. Babies continued to act as if mouth noises were acceptable associates to objects on the test trials, looking at the target significantly more than at the non-target. These results, therefore, appear to support the domain-general associative hypothesis that infants will initially accept any stimulus as a word.

Before we can conclude this, however, it may be the case that this experiment presented a less stringent test of this hypothesis than those that have been carried out previously. Perhaps the use of mouth noises that are actually phonemes in other languages (clicks exist in African languages and "psst" is a phoneme of Greek) does not stretch the bounds of the potential associates that children might accept. Recall that in the studies reviewed above, children who were 6 months older still allowed pictograms and melodies to serve as labels.

Nonetheless, the present experiment was a difficult task since it used objects of equal salience. Without the cue of perceptual salience, children must first ascertain *which* object is being labeled before they can work at learning the novel label. Even without perceptual salience on their side, and even in a task where adults are labeling an object in which babies may not be particularly interested, infants seem to assume that nonwords—sounds produced by the mouth—can map onto objects. In other words, the fact that children could learn "labels" in this experiment, even though they were mouth noises, is impressive. We are still left, therefore, with the problem of conclusively deciding whether the domain-general associative hypothesis is correct. On the one hand, mouth noises may have been too much like language and that may account for their parallel treatment to words. On the other hand, the fact that 12-month-old infants were able to learn them in an arguably more difficult word learning situation than has been used in prior studies suggests that perhaps any nonlinguistic auditory stimulus can serve as a label. To distinguish between these possible explanations, a further experiment was conducted, this time with object sounds.

EXPERIMENT 11: DIGITIZED OBJECT SOUNDS DO NOT SERVE AS LABELS FOR 12-MONTH-OLDS

The sounds that objects make do not resemble the phonemes of human speech. Would infants readily map these object noises onto an object if the social situation dictates? If they can, the domain-general associative hypothesis will gain support. If object noises are not hooked up to objects as if they are labels, however, then even 12-month-olds may be revealing a preference for human speech and speechlike sounds as labels for objects in a word learning situation in which all the cues are not in alignment. Thus, Experiment 11 used exactly the same situation as that used in Experiment 10. That is, the cues of eye gaze and handling accompanied the training phase. The only difference was in the stimuli used as "labels." In this experiment, digitized sounds served as the functional equivalent of labels.

Method

Participants. Sixteen children (half boys and half girls) composed the final sample. The age range was 11.26 to 13.23 ($M = 12.512$, $SD = 0.595$). A total of four additional participants (20%) were lost due to fussiness and experimenter error.

Procedure and stimuli. The procedure was identical to that used in Experiments 7 (words) and 10 (mouth noises) except for the use of object noises. A small hand-held electronic pen, commercially available, produced these digitized sounds. The experimenter would hold the pen, out of sight, behind and in the top-center of the display board. In this manner, the sounds appeared to be emanating from the experimenter. The two sounds selected were a beeping sound and a boink sound (of the kind heard in animated cartoons). They were produced in place of the label, in all phases. For example, a child might hear in the test phase, "Look at the [boink, boink]! See the [boink, boink]?"

Results

Overall analysis. Again, Table 4 depicts the mean looking times to the equally salient objects at all phases. A repeated-measures three-way (phase: salience/training/test) ANOVA was run. It yielded a significant main effect of phase, $F(2,30) = 52.483$, $MSE = 0.498$, $p < .0001$. To complement this analysis, we applied a one-sample test against the chance level of .50 to each of the phases.

Salience trials. Once again the objects were found to be of equivalent salience. The one-sample analysis against the chance level of .50 was not significant, $t(15) = 0.182$, $p = .429$.

Training trials. Children watched the target object significantly more than the non-target when the target was labeled with object noises, $t(15) = 14.163$, $p < .0001$, $d = 3.54$. Notice that this effect size for training is one of the largest in the experiments reported.

Test trials. Children did not, however, look proportionately more at the targeted object during test trials, $t(15) = 0.841$, $p = .2069$, $d = 0.21$. Therefore, children did not attach the object noises to the toys.

Discussion

This experiment examined whether infants would just as readily attach object noises to objects as they did mouth noises. Once again, the object noises were presented in the Interactive IPLP, a social, word learning situation. The objects used proved to be of equal salience, as anticipated. Furthermore, the time children spent looking at the target object during the training phase was significantly longer than the time spent looking at the non-target. Thus, object noises did not disrupt the training of the "labels." So far it appeared that object noises made fine labels. In stark contrast, however, to the results presented with mouth noises, infants now failed to allow object noises to function as labels. During the test trials, they did not look at the target when it was requested by its object noise any more than they looked at the non-target. This finding presents a problem for domain-general views of early word learning. Infants are not using sounds as labels. That is, they appear to be sensitive to linguistic cues, possessing domain-specific knowledge about the properties of speech.

It could be argued that this negative result was due to the "oddness" of the sounds. Infants might not want to pay attention to these infrequently heard sounds. One would be hard pressed, however, to argue that mouth noises used in the last experiment are more frequent than the digitized sounds which appear in mobiles above the crib and even in children's books. Thus, it seems implausible that the object sound results can be easily dismissed.

Woodward's (1999) social explanation also cannot account for this finding. If children are willing to learn any "label" presented in a word learning situation, then the object noises should have been treated just like the mouth noises. They were not. Instead, the object noises provide a different pattern of results despite the fact that children looked at the target during the training and had full access to the social cues.

As in the tone experiments reported by Xu (1998) and Balaban and Waxman (1997), this study demonstrates that young word learners can distinguish between object noises on the one hand and mouth noises and words on the other. Like Balaban and Waxman (1997), who found that content-filtered speech functioned more like a word than did a tone, we found that mouth noises but not object sounds operate like words. It appears that in more difficult word learning tasks, words and languagelike sounds produced by the mouth may be privileged for attaching to referents.

If neither the social explanation nor the domain-general associative hypothesis holds, however, how is one to reconcile the apparently discrepant results outlined in the introduction above? Perhaps, as we suggested, an emergentist explanation is in order. That is, in order to get 12-month-olds to override their domain-specific tendencies *not* to use sounds as labels, perhaps the right combination of social and attentional factors must be present. Only when many cues are in alignment, as they apparently were in other experiments (e.g., Woodward & Hoyne, 1999) that presented but a single, salient object, did "word" learning occur with object noises. Perhaps if we added the extra cue of salience, thereby creating a "follow-in" situation, infants would be willing to accept digitized noises as "labels."

EXPERIMENT 12: MULTIPLE CUES LEAD TO 12-MONTH-OLDS' ACCEPTANCE OF OBJECT SOUNDS AS LABELS

If attentional factors, like perceptual salience, led children to accept tones, gestures, musical notes, and pictograms as labels in Woodward and Hoyne's (1999), Namy and Waxman's (1998), and Namy's (1998) studies, then adding the cue of perceptual salience (as in the coincidental condition of Experiment 3) to the procedure of Experiment 11 should get 12-month-olds to accept even object sounds as "labels." If one object is clearly more attractive than the other, and if the "label" is given 10 times, then the situation becomes an "attention-following" (Dunham et al., 1993) and a "bludgeoning" situation (as in Experiment 7), in which all cues point to attaching the novel "label" (here, an object sound) to the interesting object. If word learning is dependent on the presence of multiple, overlapping cues, then the present experiment should ensure a sound-to-object mapping if our hypothesis is correct.

Method

Participants. Twelve children (half boys and half girls) composed the sample. The age range was 12.07 to 13.23 (M = 12.576, SD = 0.53). Two additional participants (14%) were lost due to fussiness.

Procedure and stimuli. In order to create the necessary confluence of cues, this procedure was a combination of those used in the coincidental condition of Experiment 3 (unequal object salience, with two added phases: a new name phase and a recovery phase using the original novel label) and Experiment 7 ("bludgeoning"). Thus, infants saw the experimenter "label" the interesting object 10 times while handling it. In this manner, all of the cues to word learning converged on a single interpretation. After the standard test phase, a new label was requested (in the new phase), and then (in a recovery phase) the original label was asked for again. As in Experiment 3, a shifting pattern of looking times would hint at word learning. That is, the introduction of a new name allowed us to distinguish between infants looking to the interesting toy simply because of its salience and infants looking to the interesting toy because they had learned a label. The same object noises were used in the place of words as in Experiment 11. Again, these object sounds were produced by a small hand-held pen, commercially available, which played six digitized sounds. The same sounds were used as in Experiment 11.

Results

Overall analysis. Mean looking time to the interesting and boring toys is presented in Table 5. A repeated-measures five-way (phase: salience/ training/test/new/recovery trial) ANOVA was run. It yielded a significant main effect of phase, $F(4,18) = 9.23$, $MSE = 0.415$, $p = .0001$. To decompose this effect, we analyzed each set of trials separately as in the previous experiments.

Salience trials. These results were tested against a theoretical chance level of .50. Infants looked more at the object we considered interesting, $t(11) = 3.324$, $p < .05$, $d = 0.51$.

Training trials. A one-sample analysis tested against a theoretical chance level of .50 revealed that infants looked at the interesting toy significantly longer, $t(11) = 29.32$, $p < .0001$, $d = 7.67$. This effect size is the largest observed in the training trials.

TABLE 5

EXPERIMENT 12 (HANDLING, EYE GAZE, SALIENCE, AND 10 "LABELS"—OBJECT SOUNDS): MEAN LOOKING TIME (*SD*) IN SECONDS AS A FUNCTION OF PHASE

	Salience	Training	Test	New	Recovery
Coincidental					
Interesting	2.90 (0.74)	16.15 (3.52)	2.90 (0.82)	1.05 (0.74)	1.98 (1.25)
Boring	1.88 (0.34)	1.95 (1.14)	1.32 (0.59)	2.06 (1.02)	0.90 (0.60)
% to Int.	60.7*	89.2**	68.7*	33.7*	68.7*

Note.—Planned contrasts against a theoretical chance value of 50% were used, *$p < .05$, **$p < .01$.

Test trials. As Tables 3 and 5 show, children responded in the test trials just as they had done in Experiment 3. They looked at the interesting toy longer than they looked at the boring toy. When another name was used on the new name trial, infants looked less at the interesting object. Visual fixation then increased on the recovery trial when the original "label" was requested. A repeated-measures three-way (phase: test/ new/recovery) ANOVA was run. It yielded a main effect of phase, $F(2,26) = 5.243$, $MSE = 0.132$. Subsequent Scheffe's post hoc tests demonstrated that these results were due to differences between the new phase and all other phases (critical difference = .67, test vs. new name mean difference = 2.64, $d = 0.66$, recovery trial vs. new name mean difference = 2.14, $d = .70$).

Discussion

The purpose of Experiment 12 was to understand 12-month-olds' apparently discrepant responses in Experiments 10 and 11. In Experiment 10, babies learned to attach mouth noises to objects; in Experiment 11, babies failed to attach object noises to objects. To understand this discrepancy, we posited that Experiment 11 did not provide young word learners with sufficient support to allow them to *override* any domain-specific knowledge they had about words to attach an object noise to a referent. Our prediction was that 12-month-olds would, with enough support from attentional and social cues, attach a novel sound to the most interesting object even if it was not a label per se but an object noise. Indeed, children's attention to the interesting object (the target) declined on the new name trial and then increased on the recovery trial. It was as if children were pulled off the target when they heard a new sound and pulled back to the target when they again heard the original sound. Thus, it appears the emergentist hypothesis is correct: Young word learners will accept object noises as "labels" if they are given enough attentional and social support. These findings suggest that being present in a word learning situation is not enough to learn a label (as other experiments in this *Monograph* also suggest); nor is the child operating in a purely domain-general way, willing to associate any sound with an object. Only when the cues are "piled onto" the target object will young children override their tendency to attach only speech or speechlike mouth sounds to objects.

OVERALL DISCUSSION

The studies in this chapter were designed to investigate whether word learning starts out as a mainly domain-general associative process (a "goes with" relation) that only later turns into a linguistically specific process (a "stands for" relation). Experiments 10 and 11 asked whether any nonlinguistic stimulus would be associated with an object referent. A priori, there was reason to believe that word learning might start out as a domain-general process. Gogate and Bahrick (1998) have shown, for example, that 7-month-olds can learn the link between vowel sounds and objects when the object moves synchronously with the production of the sound. Stager and Werker (1997) obtained a similar finding. Eight-month-olds can associate a syllable with a moving object and recognize when the syllable changes. Given that 7- and 8-month-olds probably do not have many words in their receptive vocabularies (Fenson et al., 1994), learning the linkage between linguistic sounds and objects must begin as a purely associative process. At some later point, however, these linguistic links turn into "real" words that carry meaning and represent a referent even in its absence. A word can even represent a category of referents rather than just the original exemplar. When this happens, the word can be said to have a "stands for" relation to what it represents. In the emergentist model, this shift is perceived as a change in weighting: from perceptual cues toward the more abstract and subtle (yet more consistent) social, linguistic, and functional aspects of meaning. Thus, for example, an infant's initial conception of the word "chair" might be tied to specific instances or some perceptually based generalizations. Over time, however, as many different kinds of chairs are seen and labeled, the strongest, most consistent mappings, those of function (something to sit on) and linguistic class (count noun used with the verb sit), come to dominate.

Trying to discover when words reach this privileged status is not an easy task. Studies just beginning to address this issue have been mainly of two types: Either they present their stimuli in the context of a socially interactive, word learning situation, or they use a habituation design where words (and nonlinguistic stimuli) co-occur with objects or representations of objects such as slides. We began by arguing that only situations that present words and nonlinguistic sounds in socially interactive word learning tasks are comparable. For this reason, we used the Interactive IPLP to see if we could get 12-month-old novice word learners to learn nonlinguistic sounds in exactly the same situation in which they learned words.

The argument that word learning starts out mainly as a domain-general associative process was an argument we were prepared to make. Judging from the results of Woodward and Hoyne (1999), we thought that both mouth noises and object noises would be learned equally well in this paradigm. To our surprise, we found a difference in these two kinds of stimuli. Mouth noises were learned as "labels"; object noises were not. Given that the situations in which these noises were offered was identical, it must be the way the children perceived the noises themselves that made the difference. Therefore, we found an unanticipated precocity in the way that children attach "labels" to referents. By 12 months of age, it appears that children are already distinguishing between noises that might be words (noises produced by the mouth) and noises that may not be words in any of the world's languages (object noises). Onomatopoeia notwithstanding, the noises that objects make are not good candidates for labels, aside from the fact that the mouth does not produce them. Apparently, by 12 months of age, babies already know that sounds that do not emanate from the mouth are a bad bet to serve as labels.

Note that the argument that babies hold out for sounds produced by the mouth requires one more experiment before it can be accepted. The mouth noises used here were arguably close to linguistic sounds given that they can appear in other languages. Although babies have lost their sensitivity to nonnative phonemes by the time they were tested (Werker & Tees, 1984), they may still recognize that these could be sounds in other languages and therefore are good label candidates. To see if this is true, further experiments must be conducted. Sounds produced by the mouth that are clearly *not* linguistic—such as burps, sneezes, raspberries, and imitations of bird chirps—should be used as stimuli. It may turn out that 12-month-olds have even finer sensibilities than we imagined; perhaps only certain kinds of mouth noises—those resembling language sounds— will work as labels at 12 months.

We found, unlike Woodward and Hoyne (1999), that babies would not connect object noises to referents as labels in Experiment 11. The explanation for these contradictory results appears to lay in these studies' task demands. Woodward and Hoyne presented the child with a single, salient object. Experiment 11 presented the child with two objects. More difficult tasks necessitate a higher level of attentional focus. In other words, it is not clear whether children were really tuned in to the adult's referential intention when they learned words in the easier, single object experiments. They may simply have been drawn by the perceptual salience of the single, novel object, which was, after all, the only potential referent in sight. Moore et al. (1999) voiced the same criticism when they discussed prior studies that attempted to manipulate adult referential cues in a situation with a single object:

> It may be that both context and the adult's referential behavior serve to focus the child's attention . . . on the intended object or event, thereby making it more salient to the child. If so, then *the acquisition of the novel word may occur through the child mapping the word on to the most salient object or event without the child being aware of the adult's referential intention.* To be clear, the point here is not that children are merely associating the new word with the most salient object. Young children are sensitive to the referential behavior of adults, but

this sensitivity may not entail an understanding that adults intend to refer to referents. Rather the idea is that a sensitivity to the referential behavior of adults may lead children to focus their own attention on the appropriate targets. (pp. 60–61)

In evaluating the different task demands, the seemingly discrepant findings between Experiment 11 and Woodward and Hoyne's (1999) findings converge. In the latter study, infants may attach object sounds (such as a whistle) to an object because of the interaction of redundant cues. In the terms of the emergentist coalition model, in Woodward and Hoyne, all the cues are in alignment and may sway children to associate any label with an object. In Experiment 11, a more difficult word learning situation that forces the child to take the referential intention of the speaker into account, object noises are not considered good candidate labels. In Experiment 12, however, when all of the cues converged, 12-month-olds appeared to use an object sound as a label.

This interpretation suggests three important conclusions: First, it is attentional focus that stands at the core of infants' early ability to associate labels and objects. Children who are learning their first words need to have multiple cues that focus their attention or they simply will not learn to associate labels with objects (as Experiments 4 through 6 and 8 attest). This attentional focus can be achieved in a number of different ways, however. As we have repeatedly seen in the studies reported throughout this *Monograph*, infants will allocate more attention if they find something perceptually salient, if they have enough time on task, or if they hear the pairing enough times.

Second, words and sounds produced by the mouth seem to be privileged in word learning. In Experiment 12, where "word" learning did occur with object sounds, we had to reintroduce perceptual salience to make it happen. Therefore, to get a baby to learn an object noise as a label, one needs to go to greater lengths than to get them to learn words or mouth noises. Part of this may be due to their familiarity with words and things emanating from the mouth. The mere mention of a word helps to heighten children's attention to available objects. As Baldwin and Markman (1989) have shown, 10- to 14-month-old infants look longer at toys presented with word labels than at objects accompanied by silence. Tones do offer some attentional stimulation, but words, perhaps because they are more frequent, have a privileged status.

The final conclusion this interpretation suggests is that the methodologies used to study word learning can influence our interpretations of what babies know. If we are to understand whether babies are capable of reading adults' referential intents, we must make our tasks sufficiently demanding so that mere associative learning will not suffice. The implication is that the findings of Woodward and Hoyne (1999) with younger children may not be tapping sufficiently into word learning processes but more into lower level associative processes fueled by children's attention to the only object available. Tasks that study word learning should push the child to go beyond the characteristics of the "attention-grabbing" stimulus to the referential intent of the speaker. Unless our tasks do that, we cannot know, as Moore et al. (1999) point out, whether children are recruiting the adults' referential behaviors for word learning—behaviors that we have found they are surely sensitive to—or just "focus[ing] their own attention on the appropriate targets" (p. 61). In this sense, it can be argued that experiments which present a single, salient stimulus are inadvertently creating an attention-following situation (Dunham et al., 1993).

In sum, these studies, coupled with others in the literature, suggest that the allocation of attention is critical in infants' first word learning. Despite domain-specific knowledge about the properties of words, under the right circumstances, infants will learn any sound to object pairing, if the attentional demands are simple enough. In a way, then, this claim comes down to the hypothesis that we began with: Word learning may well start out as a primarily associative process. It is only when children cannot just follow attentional lures but must actually use the other available cues in the coalition (such as the social cues that signal the speaker's referential intent) that it can be said that children have moved on to a more sophisticated kind of word learning, a more mature principle of reference. Nonetheless, the experiments presented here provide compelling evidence that even 12-month-olds appear to have distinguished between words, mouth sounds, and object noises. That is, even 12-month-olds have linguistically specific knowledge of the privileged status of language.

VII. GENERAL DISCUSSION

The average person spends at least one fifth of his or her life talking. . . . Over the span of one year, the average person's words would fill 132 books each containing at least 400 pages. (Van Ekeren, 1988, p. 75)

Although we often take our language capabilities for granted, the ability to use words is far from mundane. This *Monograph* explored the multifaceted factors that coalesce to permit word learning. From the first word to the torrent of words that fills volumes, language is a product of attentional, social, and linguistic cues. It is only through studying how these cues interact in the course of development that researchers can better understand the word learning process.

To unravel the ways in which children first break through the word barrier and how they become master word learners, it was important to develop a method that traces the process of vocabulary acquisition from its inception. Toward this end, the Interactive IPLP was presented for investigating word learning across the 2nd year of life. This method works with children starting on their word learning journey as well as with expert word learners. The Interactive IPLP allows one to present children with real objects and a range of attentional, social, and linguistic cues. Unlike many other methods designed to study development, the Interactive IPLP also permits examination of these multiple cues either in isolation or in interaction. That is, one can systematically vary correlations of cues to see how they impact upon the word learning process.

In this *Monograph*, a new theory of word acquisition was also introduced, the emergentist coalition model of word learning. A fundamentally developmental account that embraces many of the strengths of existing theories, this hybrid model builds on constraints/principles approaches, social-pragmatic approaches, and associationist perspectives. The emergentist coalition model allows us to explain the developmental transitions that distinguish the novice learner, just beginning to acquire words, from the more skilled veteran. The 24-month-old "professional" word learner relies on the referential intentions of the speaker even in the face of conflicting cues (Experiment 1 and see Moore et al., 1999). Using the principle of reference as a test case, we suggested that children were sensitive to a number of different input cues that can work in concert to promote word-to-world mappings. We further hypothesized that children would differentially rely on certain cues over others in the course of development. Finally, we argued that young children just learning words would be in possession of an immature principle of reference that would be supplanted by a mature principle of reference with word learning experience. Each of these hypotheses has been investigated and supported in the course of this *Monograph.*

HYPOTHESIS 1: ARE CHILDREN SENSITIVE TO MULTIPLE CUES FOR WORD LEARNING?

In these experiments, even 12-month-old infants showed an awareness of attentional, social, and linguistic cues. That is, in chapter 4, they followed perceptual salience and possibly used it in attaching a label in the coincidental condition of Experiment 3. Chapter 5 offered testimony that 12-month-olds were aware of social cues to reference. Although they could not use these cues, individually, to assign a label to an object, these infants demonstrated their awareness of these cues, such as touching and handling, by following the experimenter's lead to the target object during training. (See also the training trials of Experiments 2 and 3 in chapter 4.) Finally, in chapter 7, 12-month-olds also exhibited sensitivity to language cues by resisting a mapping between object noises and referents, unless the full coalition of cues was available. If infants did not make a distinction between language and nonlanguage sounds, they should have learned the object noises as well as they learned the mouth noises. They did not. This result suggests that even by 12 months of age, infants may recognize that language is privileged for forming mappings. Thus, even infants at the youngest age tested showed that they were sensitive to multiple cues in the word learning situation.

HYPOTHESIS 2: ARE THE CUES IN THE COALITION GIVEN DIFFERENTIAL WEIGHTS OVER THE COURSE OF LEXICAL ACQUISITION?

The answer to this question is "yes." Relevant data come from Experiments 1 and 2. Looking across age, there is a developmental trend for the younger children to more heavily weight attentional cues while the older children preferentially rely on social cues. The performance of the

19-month-olds in Experiment 1 illuminates what happens during the transition when the attentional cues are losing their sway and social cues are coming to dominate. As children are beginning their vocabulary spurt, they seem to turn their attention to social cues. Even the subtle cue of eye gaze offers enough information to draw them away from the lure of perceptual salience and onto the speaker's perspective. At this age, however, their data still illustrate the pull of perceptual salience.

This research suggests that, although the cues for word learning are available, they are not equally accessed from the start. As was seen in Experiments 4 through 6, despite an awareness of social cues, 12-month-olds did not appear to make singular use of these in word learning. As children progress through the course of language acquisition, they learn to capitalize on different cues within the coalition to make mappings between words and referents. Importantly, however, *differential weightings do not imply weightings of zero*. That is, even the 12-month-olds did pay some attention to social eye gaze (the training phases of Experiments 2 and 3) and linguistic cues (Experiments 7 and 9) and even the 24-month-olds pay attention to perceptual salience (the salience phases of Experiments 1 and 2).

HYPOTHESIS 3: DO CHILDREN MOVE FROM AN IMMATURE TO A MATURE PRINCIPLE OF REFERENCE?

Over the course of the 2nd year of life, the principle of reference evolves from an immature to a mature state. The changing weighting of the cues across development is the foundation from which this shift occurs. The movement from an immature to a mature principle of reference entails a shift from a child-dominated perspective (i.e., what the child finds salient is the referent for the label) to a speaker-dominated perspective (i.e., what the speaker is focused on is the referent for the label). Children start out by predominantly learning words that coincide with their own perspective and are only later able to learn words for objects that are signaled from another's perspective.

The most dramatic evidence for this perspective shift comes from infants' responses in the experiments that used objects of unequal and equal salience. When experimenters labeled objects on which children were already focused, 12-month-olds learned the label, with as few as five repetitions of the label. Thus, as has often been reported for studies in which attention-following is used (e.g., Dunham et al., 1993), children can learn labels when attentional, social, and language cues all point to a particular word-to-world mapping. In this relatively simple word learning situation, infants can use the principle of reference. Studies by Woodward et al. (1994) and Schafer and Plunkett (1998) that presented only a single,

103

salient object also found word learning. Furthermore, in these situations, infants will accept any stimulus, be it a mouth noise or sound, as a label (Experiment 12).

This principle of reference, however, is very fragile. When the coalition of cues is disrupted as it is in the conflict situation of Experiments 1, 2, and 3, or in experiments that use objects of equal salience (Experiments 4–6), mapping words to objects becomes far more difficult. Neither pointing, nor touching, nor handling proved sufficient in the absence of salience cues to get 12-month-olds to attach a novel label consistently to the targeted object. Only with more repetitions of the label (as in Experiment 7) and a greater amount of time on task (Experiment 9) can 12-month-olds make a tentative link between word and object.

These results support and extend prior studies in the literature on joint attention (e.g., Tomasello & Farrar, 1986) by providing a broader explanation of the results. The reason that children profit so greatly in attention-following tasks is that they can capitalize on multiple, overlapping cues in the coalition to affix a label to a referent. When the cues are fractionated, the fragile and immature principle of reference breaks down. Thus, as in Experiments 4 through 6, when the coalition of cues are not all pointing in the same direction, and children can no longer rely on the cue of perceptual salience, children with an immature principle of reference need additional support (like that received in Experiments 7 and 9) to succeed. Additional support is not always accessible, however, to the youngest learners. As a consequence, they are incapable, or unwilling, to use eye gaze alone in assigning a word to a referent even though they are sensitive to the cue of eye gaze (Hollich, Hirsh-Pasek, & Golinkoff, 1998; see also Baldwin, 1995). Twelve-month-olds need to harness multiple cues in the coalition in service to word learning.

FUTURE DIRECTIONS

The research presented here represents a beginning attempt to chart the complex interactive processes involved in word learning across the 2nd year of life. Much more needs to be done to expand the theory so that it provides a comprehensive account of the word learning strategies that young children use to break into language and to reach the naming explosion.

1. What is the relationship between vocabulary knowledge and word learning strategies?

2. Can the emergentist coalition model explain the acquisition of other principles of word learning?

3. Can the emergentist coalition model account equally well for how children acquire verbs and adjectives? As Bloom (1974) and Nelson (1996) repeatedly point out, all types of words are represented in the child's original corpus of 50 words. Thus, any theory that focuses solely on the acquisition of nouns is limited in its applicability.

Do Differences in Vocabulary on the CDI Predict Performance in the Interactive IPLP Word Learning Tasks?

A full account of the emergentist coalition model of word learning will require assessment of children with varying levels of language competence. For example, are precocious learners who capitalize on the coalition of cues those who have larger vocabularies? And, conversely, are children who fail to readily learn words those who do not effectively utilize cues in the coalition? Do parents who provide more convergent cues have children who learn more words earlier? We have been discussing word learning strategies as if they were uniform across all children. Yet, the literature reports considerable individual variation in word learning (see Hoff-Ginsberg, 1997, for a review). One way that we hoped to tap into this variation was by administering the MacArthur Communicative Development Inventory (CDI). Perhaps there would be a relationship between communicative development as measured by the CDI and children's performance on the word learning tasks we administered. Across the 12 studies, however, there was no evidence that vocabulary size (or gender, for that matter) correlated with performance on either training or test trials. The measure used for the Interactive IPLP was a proportion between the time to the target and the time to the non-target. The measures used for the CDI were number of words comprehended at 12 months and number of words produced and comprehended at 19 and 24 months. Differences in performance in the Interactive IPLP were not related to infants' vocabulary scores.

Why did we fail to find a relationship between the CDI and the present tasks? It would seem logical, for example, to expect that children with larger vocabularies would learn words more effectively in the Interactive IPLP. Yet, there are many reasons why the predicted relationship might not hold. First, the CDI taps into static infant vocabularies, not into the *processes* that infants use to acquire those vocabularies. That is, variability in comprehension is not necessarily indicative of the strategies infants are employing in learning new words. The experiments conducted in this *Monograph* reflect process—how new words are learned—not product— the number of words a child knows. Thus, although a child with many words on the CDI could be using somewhat different word learning strategies than a child with fewer words, the word learning tasks presented here were not designed to assess individual differences. Second, the CDI is a parental report measure. Whereas these are generally reliable, they do have reporting biases that may reflect parental variability more than the child's language differences. Finally, the main reason for the lack of significant correlations may have to do with the visual fixation measure used in the Interactive IPLP. That is, it is not clear that differences in visual fixation time should be expected to relate to how many words a child knows. Is the child who watches the target 1 s more than the non-target less skilled at word learning than the child who watched the target 2 s more? This is a basic problem in all infant tests that use looking time as a dependent measure. Repeatedly, in the standard IPLP, we have failed to find a relationship between looking time and language level (Hirsh-Pasek & Golinkoff, 1996a; Golinkoff, Hirsh-Pasek, & Alioto, 1998).

Expanding the Model Beyond the Principle of Reference

The emergentist coalition model must help us explain not just the principle of reference, but also the first tier principles of extendibility and object scope in the developmental lexical principles framework (Golinkoff et al., 1994). That is, will a coalition of cues best explain the emergence and change in these principles?

Extendibility. In an evolutionary sense, extendibility is not that far from generalization. Thus, just as a rat can learn to run through any triangular-shaped door for food, so can a child "generalize" the use of the word "rabbit" to include white and black bunnies. Likewise, the ontological origins of extendibility are probably in place quite early as evidenced by children's performance on other, more traditional "generalization tasks." Thus, from the emergentist viewpoint, extendibility begins from the very basic, domain-general process of generalization and a reliance on basic perceptual similarity and temporal contiguity. Extendibility matures through guided distributional learning, however, when children discover the domain-specific manner in which words extend to include taxonomic category members. That is, children recognize that linguistic categories for nouns label objects of like kind and not objects that are used together (thematic relationships) or objects that just look alike. Thus, children might begin extension by relying on superficial, perceptual features of the object—such as shape (Landau, Smith, & Jones, 1992). They move on, however, to extensions based on taxonomic category (Golinkoff et al., 1994; Golinkoff, Shuff-Bailey, Olguin, & Ruan, 1995; Shuff & Golinkoff, 1998) when they discover the invariant manner in which a word is used across exemplars that do not share the same perceptual attributes. That is, as children hear the word "chair" used in reference to red chairs and blue chairs, lawn chairs and bean bag chairs, they become increasingly aware that taxonomic categories of objects do not necessarily share similar shape. Similarly, one can have a radio shaped like a pen, or a pen that looks like a lollipop. Hearing a word used across multiple exemplars and across multiple contexts makes children come to realize the consistent factor of extension—a factor that, for most objects, is usually function. Thus, children may move from shape-based to function-based extension as they discover that function more consistently indicates the appropriate extension. (See Hollich, 1999, for a computational model and preliminary test of this idea.)

The same three categories of cues studied for the principle of reference—attentional, social, and linguistic—seem to come into play for the principle of extendibility as well. For example, for 14-month-olds, we have found that object handling by the baby enables extension to occur (Hennon, Rocroi, & Chung, 1999). This suggests that domain-general attentional cues, heightened through haptic exploration, *do* play an important role in initial extension. Thus, for extendibility, a change is seen when the children's weightings of attentional factors like perceptual similarity shift to indices for conceptual similarity, from an emphasis on the physical features of an object to more abstract features like taxonomic category membership, as defined by function (Keil, 1989). Social cues, too, may play a role in situations where the child can observe an adult grouping objects together for functional purposes. Thus, observing an adult separate coins and paper money into a pile, physically apart from other items found in a pocketbook, may serve as a cue to babies about the fact that the diverse objects in this pile belong in the same category. Finally, linguistic cues to extendibility may gain in weight as the child matures. Naigles (1990) reports that even at 2 years of age, syntax can get children to focus on the appropriate action.

Object scope. The model also should explain the development of the principle of object scope. Object scope has two parts and we are attacking both from the emergentist coalition perspective. In its immature state, object scope first predicts that objects will be labeled over the actions in which the objects are engaged. It also predicts that labels will be taken for whole objects rather than their parts or attributes. Recent research indicates that 12-, 19-, and 24-month-olds do, in fact, make this assumption (Arnold et al., 1999). Also, experiments by Spelke (1990) seem to confirm this perceptual bias toward whole objects early in the first year of life, although children can also recognize and attend to actions and parts of objects (Younger & Cohen, 1986).

In a mature version of object scope, however, linguistic cues come to increasingly determine whether a word is taken to label the whole object or the action of the object or a property of the object. In one study,

19-month-old children could appropriately direct their attention to a whole object when asked to look at "the blick" but directed their attention to the action when "blicking" was requested (Echols, 1993). In another study, children by 25 months of age were shown to use noun syntax differentially than adjective syntax (Klibanoff & Waxman, 1999) in a word-mapping task. When asked to find a "blickish" one (instead of "a blick") children no longer selected an object in the same taxonomic category, showing that they were sensitive to the adjectival markers and syntax.

Thus, the emergentist view can be expanded to capture the development of the lexical principles of the first tier. It does this by describing how children differentially tap into a coalition of factors available in the input to construct, through guided distributional learning, ever more complex and domain-specific principles for word learning. The studies reported here also use only one type of data, behavioral data. To make the case for a shift in weights, converging evidence is critical. To further specify the mechanisms of change, we are pursuing non-behavioral approaches. Computational modeling might better elucidate the source of these changing weights and give the concept of guided distributional learning greater neurological specificity (Hollich, 1999).

Emergentist Coalition Model as Applied to Verbs

Although object words are the highest proportion of items acquired by infants breaking the language barrier, adjectives and verbs also appear in earliest vocabularies. Moreover, in the latter part of the 2nd year of life, as children begin to combine words, verbs surface as the "hero" of a sentence, critical to determining its meaning. For this reason, it would seem vital to expand the emergentist model to explain verbs and adjectives as well as nouns. This is particularly important when one considers that children's acquisition of verbs and adjectives would seem to be handicapped because most of the lexical principles appear to work against their acquisition. For example, the principle of object scope's emphasis on objects over actions would seem to prohibit easy verb learning.

Golinkoff, Hirsh-Pasek, Mervis, and Frawley (1995) posited an extension of the lexical principles framework for verbs. For example, in their framework, the principle of object scope has a counterpart in verb learning, a principle of "whole action." That is, like the principle of whole object, infants segment actions along predictable lines into what Mandler (1992) referred to as image-schemas. Furthermore, reference applies equally well to salient actions over boring actions, and extendibility can be seen for words other than nouns. This version of extendibility is evidenced by Korean children's ready overgeneralizations of their earliest spatial words (Choi & Bowerman, 1991). Similarly, Golinkoff, Jacquet, and Hirsh-Pasek

(1993) have demonstrated that a rudimentary version of their principle of novel name-nameless category is used by 34-month-olds in the acquisition of a novel label for a novel action. Thus, lexical principles would seem to apply for verbs as well as nouns.

Similarly, just as children's early acquisition of object names appears to require a confluence of factors, so, too, we expect that verb learning requires multiple cues to make the appropriate link between early verbs and their respective actions. To date, there has been relatively little research on how children learn their first action words (but see Tomasello & Merriman, 1991). Nonetheless, it is not hard to imagine that verb learning results from the combined interaction of attentional, social, and linguistic cues. For example, one study by Hirsh-Pasek and Golinkoff (1996a) confirmed that children can select the appropriate action using syntactical cues. Thus, when they hear that "Cookie Monster is squatting Big Bird," 24-month-old children will look at a display in which Cookie Monster is making Big Bird squat. These children do not know the meaning of the verb "squat" and are thereby using syntactic cues to figure out that it must be transitive and causal. By contrast, when they hear, "Cookie Monster is squatting with Big Bird," they now look at the screen where Cookie Monster and Big Bird are squatting together. Notice that it was not enough for them to understand that Cookie Monster, Big Bird, and a novel action were involved. These infants had to make use of syntactical cues in assigning the appropriate interpretation to the sentence and watching the matching screen.

SUMMARY AND CONCLUSIONS

Despite the need for further research, the emergentist coalition model has already made important strides in understanding how children acquire words. It is the first to meet the challenge of creating a model that considers the impact of multiple sources of information in solving the complex task of word learning. Many others have suggested the need for theoretical perspectives that embrace a multifactored approach (e.g., Gelman & Williams, 1998; Siegler, 1996). In 1974, Bloom cautioned against looking myopically at the form of language, the content, or its use. Language, Bloom (1993) wrote, is the "necessary integration of all three." More recently, Nelson (1996) wrote, "... there are no single effective pushes to the developing system but rather a combination of influences that lead to observable change" (p. 85). Smith and Thelen (1993; Thelen & Smith, 1994), likewise, support a dynamic systems model that talks of emergent interactive processes in language development. Finally, Karmiloff-Smith (1992) urged the field to adopt a more integrative view:

> The flourishing new domain of cognitive science needs to go beyond the
> traditional nativist-empiricist dichotomy that permeates much of the field, in
> favor of an epistemology that embraces both innate predispositions and con-
> structivism. (p. 193)

To explain early word acquisition, or any other complex behavior,
the field needs to embrace a more integrative, nonlinear view of development. From this apparent consensus and from the research reported
in this *Monograph*, we believe that four final points can be drawn. First,
no single cue, in and of itself, creates word learning. That is, multiple
cues are necessary to explain the complexity of lexical acquisition. Second, the focus in word learning research must be on process as well as
product. Third, understanding word learning requires the study of its
origins. Finally, without initial biases, the word learning seen in the expert 24-month-old would be impossible. Only a perspective that considers
all of the above can be said to fully address the word learning problem.

There Is No Single Cue to Word Learning

The *perception* of the cues in the coalition is not the same as the *use*
of those cues in service to word learning. Although babies can notice
social eye gaze (the training phases of Experiments 2, 3, and 8), this does
not mean that they will use this awareness in learning a new word (Experiments 4–6). There are a number of examples in the literature of
infants' failure to use information in one domain in the service of tasks
in another domain. For example, Stager and Werker (1997) reported that
14-month-olds seem to lose the ability to discriminate between native phonemes once word learning comes on the scene. In a task that required
babies to associate a novel syllable to a novel referent shown on video-
tape, 8-month-olds succeeded, while 14-month-olds failed! Stager and
Werker (1997) reasoned that at 14 months of age, when children are
actively engaged in word learning, they lapse in their ability to distinguish between phonemes, perhaps because so much of their attention is
allocated to learning new words. When word learning is removed from
the task because the associate for the syllable is a poor candidate for
receiving a label (a checkerboard that fills the entire screen), they now
once again reveal their ability to discriminate between phonemes. Some-
time after the vocabulary spurt, infants once again seem to be able to
coordinate phonemic discrimination and word learning (Hoskins, Golinkoff,
Chung, & Hirsh-Pasek, 1998). Similarly, Bloom (1994) finds that emotional expression is not initially coordinated with language expression.
That is, linguistic expression seems to occur when the child is expressing

neutral affect. Only later in development, at around 18 months of age, can children coordinate emotional affect with linguistic expression, even though they have been using their faces to show emotion for many months prior.

From this convergence of evidence, it appears that, for lexical acquisition, 12-month-old infants are not hampered in their ability to detect various cues. Rather, they are lacking in their ability to harness and coordinate these cues in the word learning situation. When they finally become sophisticated enough to assemble various pieces of information in a single task, the results are dramatic. Word learners move from novice to expert as the coalition of factors becomes coordinated, or, to borrow a term from dynamical systems theory, self-organized. If it is the coordination and harnessing of multiple cues that promotes word learning, then it becomes clear that there is no single smoking gun for word learning. Word learning emerges from children's consideration of multiple factors, a coalition of cues. Certain of these cues become more or less important over developmental time with word learning experience, but no cue, in and of itself, is sufficient for word learning to occur. Thus, we found that neither perceptual salience nor social eye gaze, by themselves, could produce evidence for word learning in 12-month-olds.

Focus on Process as Well as Product

Endorsing a multiply determined course of development means that it is important to study the *process* of word learning and not just the products of word learning. Less emphasis is needed on the developmental milestones of lexical acquisition (such as the age at which children have a certain number of words in their receptive vocabularies), and more emphasis is needed on the processes that enable these milestones. Sternberg (1984) put it well when he wrote,

> There are two fundamental questions in developmental psychology. First, what are the psychological states individuals pass through at different points in their development? Second, what are the mechanisms of development by which individuals pass from one state to another? A strong case could be made that the second question is the more basic one ... [yet] I doubt that as much as one percent of our developmental literature addresses the question of the mechanisms by which developmental changes are effected. (p. vii)

Under the associationist approach, there is an emphasis on the study of process rather than outcomes (e.g., see Smith, 1995) and we have adopted that emphasis as well. How do children move from one milestone to another? What prompts change in the system? Can one treat variability as a finding rather than as error? Why do young children look better or worse at word learning in the present experiments that presented different combinations of cues?

To address change, researchers will have to look microscopically at the variables under study. This research is expensive both in time and in money, but it is only under this closer look that we can discover shifts in process over time—such as differential reliance on attentional, social, and linguistic cues for word learning. Longitudinal analyses like those performed by Thelen and Smith (1994) and Siegler (1996) offer compelling tests of such processes. These can then be modeled in computer simulations like those of Hollich (1999), Plunkett (1997), or Smith (1995), which alter word learning strategies over time by computing differential weights across varied input.

Understanding Word Learning Requires the Study of Its Origins

The move to a process model of word learning raises a third point: The field must study word learning processes in children who are just beginning to break the language barrier. As we have demonstrated in this *Monograph*, word learning undergoes dramatic changes in the 2nd year of life. With few exceptions, such as those of Waxman and her colleagues (e.g., Waxman & Markow, 1995), Woodward and her colleagues (Woodward et al., 1994), or Schafer and Plunkett (1998), the bulk of our word learning data comes from studies of children above 18 months of age. Yet, 18-month-olds have participated in the word learning game for at least 6 months. They are on the doorstep of the vocabulary spurt. Although these studies on 18-month-olds have presented a wealth of data, one cannot assume that 18-month-old behavior speaks to word learning capacities of the 12-month-old. Just as it would be unfair to attribute the 3-year-old's grammatical ability to the neonate, it is unfair to credit the 12-month-old with the ability to read the intent that lies behind the uttered word.

To be sure, one of the problems the field often encountered was a methodological one. It has been difficult to construct controlled language learning tasks that assess the development of a child's first words. New tests of early word learning, however, circumvent some of these earlier hurdles. With methods like Waxman and Markow's (1995) haptic habituation task, Gogate and Bahrick's (1998) intermodal habituation task, the original IPLP (e.g., Schafer & Plunkett, 1998; Golinkoff, Hirsh-Pasek, & Alioto, 1998), and the Interactive IPLP presented here, the methodological gaps can be filled. Word learning can now be studied from its inception. Furthermore, the same methods can be used to follow the children longitudinally and to see whether the word learning process changes over time. A developmental view of word learning, although essential, has been frequently lacking.

Initial Biases Must Exist

A serious longitudinal, developmental view also causes researchers to grapple with the origins of the word learning principles. If it is true, as the old adage goes, that "you can't get something from nothing," then as Macnamara (1982) wrote, it is hard to imagine how children would acquire a principle like reference if they did not start out with one. For Macnamara, reference is a primitive. Why ever assume that sounds go with objects? How could a child progress from pure association to symbolic thought? If there were not a principle like reference, why would children ever assume that the social partner is referring in the first place? The constraints/principles view solves this problem as Macnamara did by claiming that reference is in the head of the beholder. This is not to say that the child is uninfluenced by social input, just that this input would be irrelevant if reference was not present in some form in the first place.

Children may have a principle that guides them to attach sound to object, action, and event but not know the specifics of word-to-world mapping. In the emergentist coalition model, children begin with what we call an immature principle of reference that is informed by many inputs—including attentional, social, and linguistic cues. Gradually, as they process these inputs using guided distributional learning, they mold that principle into one that assists them in word learning and that resembles the principles used as adults. Small biases in development can give rise to large differences in final behavior.

Final Conclusions

Some might argue that a hybrid view is merely an attempt to be all things to all people, that it is not a parsimonious account of word learning. The present studies do more, however, than pay lip service to the fact that various cues interact to create word learning. In the prior study of word learning, competing explanations have often been invoked to explain results. Yet, the facts do not distinguish between such "competing" theories because these theories are not truly in competition. The associationist, social-pragmatic, and constraints/principles views are not incompatible with each other. Rather, they are *incomplete* without each other. The emergentist coalition model is the most parsimonious account that fully captures the multifaceted nature of lexical acquisition. This model unifies the many theories of word learning into a single explanation and

113

provides the common ground on which attentional, social, and linguistic evidence can be considered. Although this model is only in its infancy, this *Monograph* demonstrated that children are sensitive to many different sources of information and will change their weightings of these sources at different times in development and in different contexts. Children need attentional and social cues as well as conceptual constraints to overcome the word learning problem, much as a baker needs multiple ingredients to make a cake. And just as in the culinary arts, the end result is more than any of one of its constituent parts.

REFERENCES

Adamson, L. B. (1995). *Communication development during infancy.* Madison, WI: Brown & Benchmark.

Akhtar, N., Carpenter, M., & Tomasello, M. (1996). The role of discourse novelty in early word learning. *Child Development, 67*, 635–645.

Akhtar, N., Dunham, F., & Dunham, P. J. (1991). Directive interactions and early vocabulary development: The role of joint attentional focus. *Journal of Child Language, 18*, 41–49.

Akhtar, N., & Montague, L. (1999). Early lexical acquisition: The role of cross-situational learning. *First Language, 19*, 347–358.

Akhtar, N., & Tomasello, M. (1996). Twenty-four-month-old children learn words for absent objects and actions. *British Journal of Developmental Psychology, 14*, 79–93.

Anselmi, D., Tomasello, M., & Acunzo, M. (1986). Young children's responses to neutral and specific contingent queries. *Journal of Child Language, 13*, 135–144.

Arnold, K., Golinkoff, R., Hirsh-Pasek, K., Driscoll, K., Rocroi, C., & Hollich, G. (1999, November). *The whole is greater than the sum of the parts: Investigating the object scope principle.* Paper presented at the meeting of the Boston University Conference on Language Development, Boston, MA.

Aslin, R. N., Jusczyk, P. W., & Pisoni, D. B. (1998). Speech and auditory processing during infancy: Constraints on and precursors to language. In D. Kuhn & R. Siegler (Eds.), *Handbook of child psychology: Vol. 2. Cognition, perception and language.* New York: Wiley.

Aslin, R. N., Saffran, J. R., & Newport, E. L. (1998). Computation of conditional probability statistics by 8-month-old infants. *Psychological Science, 9*, 321–324.

Bahrick, L. E. (1983). Infants' perception of substance and temporal synchrony in multimodal events. *Infant Behavior and Development, 6*, 429–451.

Balaban, M., & Waxman, S. (1997). Do word labels facilitate categorization in 9-month-old infants? *Journal of Experimental Child Psychology, 64*, 3–26.

Baldwin, D. A. (1989). Priorities in children's expectations about object label reference: Form over color. *Child Development, 60*, 1289–1306.

Baldwin, D. A. (1991). Infants' contribution to the achievement of joint reference. *Child Development, 62*, 875–890.

Baldwin, D. A. (1993). Infants' ability to consult the speaker for clues to word reference. *Journal of Child Language, 20*, 394–419.

Baldwin, D. A. (1995). Understanding the link between joint attention and language. In C. Moore & P. J. Dunham (Eds.), *Joint attention: Its origins and role in development.* Hillsdale, NJ: Erlbaum.

Baldwin, D. A., Brigitte, B., & Lenna, O. (1997). *Gaze-checking as a response to communicative ambiguity in 12- and 18-month-olds.* Unpublished manuscript, University of Oregon.

Baldwin, D. A., & Markman, E. M. (1989). Establishing word-object relations: A first step. *Child Development,* **60,** 381–398.

Baldwin, D. A., Markman, E. M., Bill, B., Desjardins, N., Irwin, J. M., & Tidball, G. (1996). Infants' reliance on a social criterion for establishing word-object relations. *Child Development,* **67,** 3135–3153.

Baldwin, D. A., & Tomasello, M. (1998). Word learning: A window on early pragmatic understanding. In E. V. Clark (Ed.), *Proceedings of the Stanford Child Language Research Forum.* Stanford, CA: Center for the Study of Language and Information.

Barrett, M. D. (1978). Lexical development and overextension in child language. *Journal of Child Language,* **5,** 205–219.

Bates, E., & MacWhinney, B. (1987). Competition, variation, and language learning. In B. MacWhinney (Ed.), *Mechanisms of language acquisition.* Hillsdale, NJ: Lawrence Erlbaum.

Bernstein-Ratner, N. (1986). Durational cues which mark clause boundaries in mother-child speech. *Journal of Phonetics,* **14,** 303–309.

Bloom, L. (1973). *One word at a time: The use of single word utterances before syntax.* The Hague: Mouton.

Bloom, L. (1974). Talking, understanding and thinking: Developmental relationship between receptive and expressive language. In R. L. Schiefelbusch & L. Lloyd (Eds.), *Language perspectives—Acquisition, retardation and intervention.* Baltimore: University Park Press.

Bloom, L. (1993). *The transition from infancy to language: Acquiring the power of expression.* New York: Cambridge University Press.

Bloom, P. (1994). Possible names: The role of syntax-semantics mappings in the acquisition of nominals. *Lingua,* **92,** 297–329.

Butterworth, G., & Grover, L. (1990). Joint visual attention, manual pointing, and preverbal communication in human infancy. In M. Jeannerod (Ed.), *Attention and performance XIII.* Hillsdale, NJ: Erlbaum.

Carey, S. (1978). The child as word learner. In M. Halle, J. Bresnan, & G. A. Miller (Eds.), *Linguistic theory and psychological reality.* Cambridge, MA: The MIT Press.

Carpenter, M., Nagell, K., & Tomasello, M. (1998). Social cognition, joint attention, and communicative competence from 9 to 15 months of age. *Monographs of the Society for Research in Child Development,* **63**(4, Serial No. 255).

Choi, S., & Bowerman, M. (1991). Learning to express motion events in English and Korean: A crosslinguistic study. *Journal of Child Language,* **22,** 497–529.

Clark, E. V. (1973). What's in a word? On the child's acquisition of semantics in his first language. In T. Moore (Ed.), *Cognitive development and the acquisition of language.* New York: Academic Press.

Clark, E. V. (1983). Meanings and concepts. In J. H. Flavell & E. M. Markman (Eds.), *Handbook of child psychology: Vol. III. Cognitive development.* New York: John Wiley & Sons.

Clark, E. V. (1993). *The lexicon in acquisition.* Cambridge, MA: Cambridge University Press.

Coldren, J. T., & Colombo, J. (1994). The nature and processes of preverbal learning. *Monographs of the Society for Research in Child Development,* **59**(4, Serial No. 241).

Corkum, V., & Moore, C. (1995). Development of joint visual attention in infants. In C. Moore & P. J. Dunham (Eds.), *Joint attention: Its origins and role in development.* Hillsdale, NJ: Lawrence Erlbaum.

Deacon, T. W. (1997). *The symbolic species: The co-evolution of language and the brain.* New York: W. W. Norton.

Diesendruck, G., Gelman, S. A., & Lebowitz, K. (1998). Conceptual and linguistic biases in children's word learning. *Developmental Psychology,* **34**(5), 823–839.

Dromi, E. (1987). *Early lexical development.* Cambridge, UK: Cambridge University Press.

Dunham, P. J., Dunham, F., & Curwin, A. (1993). Joint-attentional states and lexical acquisition at 18 months. *Developmental Psychology,* **29**(5), 827–831.

Echols, C. H. (1991, April). *Infants' attention to objects and consistency in linguistic and nonlinguistic contexts.* Paper presented at the Biennial Meeting of the Society for Research in Child Development, Seattle, WA.

Echols, C. H. (1993, April). *Attentional predispositions and linguistic sensitivity in the acquisition of object words.* Paper presented at the Biennial Meeting of the Society for Research in Child Development, New Orleans, LA.

Echols, C. H. (1998, April). *The identification of words and their meanings in the transition into language.* Paper presented at the International Conference on Infant Studies, Atlanta, GA.

Elman, J. L., Bates, E. A., Johnson, M., Karmiloff-Smith, A., Parisi, D., & Plunkett, K. (1996). *Rethinking innateness: A connectionist perspective on development.* Cambridge, MA: MIT Press.

Fagan, J. (1971). Infant recognition memory for a series of visual stimuli. *Journal of Experimental Child Psychology,* **11**, 244–250.

Fagan, J., Singer, L., Montie, J., & Shepard, P. (1986). Selective screening device for the early detection of normal or delayed cognitive development in infants at risk for later mental retardation. *Pediatrics,* **78**, 1021–1026.

Fenson, L., Dale, P., Reznick, S., Bates, E., Thai, D., & Pethick, S. (1994). Variability in early communicative development. *Monographs of the Society for Research in Child Development,* **59**(5, Serial No. 242).

Fernald, A., McRoberts, G., & Herrera, C. (in press). Effects of prosody and word position on lexical comprehension in infants. *Journal of Experimental Psychology.*

Flavell, J. H., Friedrichs, A. G., & Hoyt, J. D. (1970). Developmental changes in memorization processes. *Cognitive Psychology,* **1**, 324–340.

Flom, R. A., Phill, C. G., Pick, A. D., & Burch, M. (1999, April). *Attention following and attention switching revisited: 18-month-olds' ability to learn novel labels.* Paper presented at the meeting of the Society for Research in Child Development, Albuquerque, NM.

Franco, F., & Butterworth, G. (1996). Pointing and social awareness: Declaring and requesting in the second year. *Journal of Child Language,* **23**, 307–336.

Gelman, R., & Greeno, J. G. (1989). On the nature of competence: Principles for understanding in a domain. In L. B. Resnick (Ed.), *Knowing and learning: Essays in honor of Robert Glaser.* Hillsdale, NJ: Erlbaum.

Gelman, R., & Williams, E. M. (1998). Enabling constraints for cognitive development and learning: Domain specificity and epigenesis. In W. Damon (Ed.), *Handbook of child psychology: Vol 2. Cognition, perception, and language.* New York: Wiley.

Gelman, S. A. (1987). Young children's inductions from natural kinds: The role of categories and appearances. *Child Development,* **58**, 1532–1540.

Gelman, S. A., Croft, W., Fu, P., Clausner, T., & Gottfried, G. (1998). Why is a pomegranate an apple? The role of shape, taxonomic relatedness, and prior lexical knowledge in children's overextensions of apple and dog. *Journal of Child Language,* **25**, 267–291.

Gelman, S. A., & Taylor, M. (1984). How two-year-old children interpret proper and common names for unfamiliar objects. *Child Development,* **55**, 1535–1540.

Gogate, L. J., & Bahrick, L. E. (1998). Intersensory redundancy facilitates learning of arbitrary relations between vowel sounds and objects in seven-month-old infants. *Journal of Experimental Child Psychology,* **69**, 133–149.

Goldfield, B. A., & Reznick, S. (1990). Early lexical acquisition: Rate, content and the vocabulary spurt. *Journal of Child Language,* **17**, 171–183.

Golinkoff, R. M., & Hirsh-Pasek, K. (1995). Reinterpreting children's sentence comprehension: Toward a new framework. In P. Fletcher & B. MacWhinney (Eds.), *The handbook of child language*. London: Blackwell.

Golinkoff, R. M., Hirsh-Pasek, K., & Alioto, A. (1998). *Infants learn lexical items better in infant-directed than in adult-directed speech*. Unpublished manuscript, University of Delaware.

Golinkoff, R. M., Hirsh-Pasek, K., Bailey, L. M., & Wenger, N. R. (1992). Young children and adults use lexical principles to learn new nouns. *Developmental Psychology*, **28**, 99–108.

Golinkoff, R., Hirsh-Pasek, K., Cauley, K. M., & Gordon, L. (1987). The eyes have it: Lexical and syntactic comprehension in a new paradigm. *Journal of Child Language*, **14**, 23–45.

Golinkoff, R. M., Hirsh-Pasek, K., & Hollich, G. (1999). Emerging cues for early word learning. In B. MacWhinney (Ed.), *The emergence of language*. Hillsdale, NJ: Erlbaum.

Golinkoff, R. M., Hirsh-Pasek, K., Mervis, C. B. & Frawley, W. B. (1995). Lexical principles can be extended to the acquisition of verbs. In W. E. Merriman & Michael Tomasello (Eds.), *Beyond names for things: Young children's acquisition of verbs*. Hillsdale, NJ: Lawrence Erlbaum Associates.

Golinkoff, R. M., Hirsh-Pasek, K., & Schweisguth, M. A. (in press). A reappraisal of young children's knowledge of grammatical morphemes. In J. Weissenborn & B. Hoehle (Eds.), *Approaches to bootstrapping: Phonological, syntactic and neurophysiological aspects of early language acquisition*. Amsterdam-Philadelphia: John Benjamins.

Golinkoff, R. M., Jacquet, R., & Hirsh-Pasek, K. (1993). *Lexical principles underlie verb learning*. Unpublished manuscript.

Golinkoff, R. M., Mervis, C., & Hirsh-Pasek, K. (1994). Early object labels: The case for a developmental lexical principles framework. *Journal of Child Language*, **21**, 125–155.

Golinkoff, R. M., Shuff-Bailey, M., Olguin, M., & Ruan, W. (1995). Young children extend novel words at the basic level: Evidence for the principle of categorical scope. *Developmental Psychology*, **31**, 494–507.

Hall, D. G., Waxman, S. R., & Hurwitz, W. M. (1993). How two- and four-year-old children interpret adjectives and count nouns. *Child Development*, **64**, 1651–1664.

Hebb, D. O. (1949). *The organization of behavior: A neuropsychological theory*. New York: John Wiley.

Hennon, E., Rocroi, C., & Chung, H. (1999, April). *Testing the principle of extendibility: Are new words learned as proper nouns or category labels?* Paper presented at the meeting of the Society for Research in Child Development, Albuquerque, NM.

Hermer, L., & Spelke, E. (1996). Modularity and development: The case of spatial reorientation. *Cognition*, **61**, 195–232.

Hirsh-Pasek, K., & Golinkoff, R. M. (1991). Language comprehension: A new look at some old themes. In N. Krasnegor, D. Rumbaugh, M. Studdert-Kennedy, & R. Schiefelbusch (Eds.), *Biological and behavior determinants of language development*. Hillsdale, NJ: Erlbaum.

Hirsh-Pasek, K., & Golinkoff, R. M. (1993). Skeletal supports for grammatical learning: What infants bring to the language learning task. In C. Rovee-Collier (Ed.), *Advances in infancy research* (Vol. 8). Norwood, NJ: Ablex.

Hirsh-Pasek, K., & Golinkoff, R. M. (1996a). *The origins of grammar: Evidence from early language comprehension*. Cambridge, MA: MIT Press.

Hirsh-Pasek, K., & Golinkoff, R. M. (1996b). The preferential looking paradigm reveals emerging language comprehension. In D. McDaniel, C. McKee, & H. Cairns (Eds.), *Methods for assessing children's syntax*. Cambridge, MA: MIT Press.

Hirsh-Pasek, K., Golinkoff, R. M., & Hollich, G. (in press). An emergentist coalition model for word learning: Mapping words to objects is a product of the interaction of multiple cues. In R. M. Golinkoff, K. Hirsh-Pasek, N. Akhtar, L. Bloom, G. Hollich,

L. Smith, M. Tomasello, & A. Woodward, *Becoming a word learner: A debate on lexical acquisition.* New York: Oxford Press.

Hoff-Ginsberg, E. (1997). *Language development.* London: Routledge.

Hollich, G. (1999). *Mechanisms of word learning: A computational model.* Unpublished doctoral dissertation, Temple University, Philadelphia, PA.

Hollich, G., Hirsh-Pasek, K., & Golinkoff, R. M. (1998). Introducing the 3-D intermodal preferential looking paradigm: A new method to answer an age-old question. In C. Rovee-Collier (Ed.), *Advances in infancy research* (Vol. 12). Norwood, NJ: Ablex.

Hollich, G., Hirsh-Pasek, K., Tucker, M., & Golinkoff, R. (2000). A change is afoot: Emergentist thinking in language acquisition. In P. B. Anderson (Ed.), *Downward causation.* Aarhus: Aarhus University Press.

Hoskins, S., Golinkoff, R. M., Chung, H., & Hirsh-Pasek, K. (1998, June). *Thirty-two to thirty-five-month-olds can discriminate novel minimal pairs.* Paper presented at the American Psychological Society.

Huttenlocher, J., & Smiley, P. (1987). Early word meanings: The case of object names. *Cognitive Psychology, 19,* 63–89.

Jusczyk, P. W. (1997). *The discovery of spoken language.* Cambridge, MA: MIT Press.

Jusczyk, P. W., & Aslin, R. N. (1995). Infants' detection of the sound patterns of words in fluent speech. *Cognitive Psychology, 29,* 1–23.

Jusczyk, P. W., Cutler, A., & Redanz, N. J. (1993). Infants' preference for the predominant stress patterns of English words. *Child Development, 64,* 675–687.

Karmiloff-Smith, A. (1992). *Beyond modularity: A developmental perspective on cognitive science.* Cambridge, MA: MIT Press.

Katz, N., Baker, E., & Macnamara, J. (1974). What's in a name? A study of how children learn common and proper names. *Child Development, 50,* 1–13.

Keil, F. C. (1989). *Concepts, kinds and cognitive development.* Cambridge, MA: MIT Press.

Kellman, P., & Arterberry, M. E. (1998). *The cradle of knowledge: Development of perception in infancy.* Cambridge, MA: MIT Press.

Kellman, P., & Spelke, E. (1983). Perception of partially occluded objects. *Cognitive Psychology, 15,* 483–524.

Kemler Nelson, D. G. (1995). Principle-based inferences in young children's categorization: Revisiting the impact of function on the naming of artifacts. *Cognitive Development, 10,* 347–380.

Keppel, G. (1991). *Design and analysis: A researcher's handbook* (3rd ed.). Englewood Cliffs, NJ: Prentice Hall.

Klibanoff, R. S., & Waxman, S. R. (1999). Preschoolers' acquisition of novel adjectives and the role of basic-level kind. In A. Greenhill, M. Hughes, H. Littlefield, & H. Walsh (Eds.), *Proceedings of the 22nd annual Boston University Conference on Language Development.* Boston, MA: Cascadilla Press.

Landau, B., Smith, L. B., & Jones, S. (1992). Syntactic context and the shape bias in children's and adults' lexical learning. *Cognitive Development, 3,* 299–321.

Leung, E. H. L., & Rheingold, H. L. (1981). Development of pointing as a social gesture. *Developmental Psychology, 17,* 215–220.

Macnamara, J. (1982). *Names for things.* Cambridge, MA: MIT Press.

Mandler, J. M. (1992). How to build a baby: 2. Conceptual primitives. *Psychological Review, 99,* 587–604.

Markman, E. M. (1987). How children constrain the possible meanings of words. In U. Neisser (Ed.), *Concepts and conceptual development: Ecological and intellectual factors in categorization.* Cambridge, MA: Cambridge University Press.

Markman, E. M. (1989). *Categorization and naming in children: Problems of induction.* Cambridge, MA: MIT Press.

Markman, E. M. (1992). Constraints on word learning: Speculations about their nature, origin, and domain specificity. In M. R. Gunnar & M. P. Maratsos (Eds.), *Minnesota Symposium on Child Psychology* (Vol. 25). Hillsdale, NJ: Erlbaum.

Markman, E. M., & Hutchinson, J. E. (1984). Children's sensitivity to constraints on word meaning: Taxonomic vs. thematic relations. *Cognitive Psychology*, **16**, 1–27.

Markman, E. M., & Wachtel, G. F. (1988). Children's use of mutual exclusivity to constrain the meaning of words. *Cognitive Psychology*, **20**, 121–157.

Masur, E. F. (1982). Mothers' responses to infants' object-related gestures: Influences on lexical development. *Journal of Child Language*, **9**, 23–30.

McShane, J. (1979). The development of naming. *Linguistics*, **17**, 879–905.

Merriman, W. E., & Bowman, L. (1989). The mutual exclusivity bias in children's early word learning. *Monographs of the Society for Research in Child Development*, **54**(3–4, Serial No. 220).

Mervis, C. B., & Bertrand, J. (1993). Acquisition of early object labels: The roles of operating principles and input. In A. P. Kaiser & D. B. Gray (Eds.), *Enhancing children's communication: Research foundations for interventions* (Vol. 2). Baltimore, MD: Brookes.

Mervis, C. B., Golinkoff, R. M., & Bertrand, J. (1994). Two-year-olds readily learn multiple labels for the same basic level category. *Child Development*, **65**, 971–991.

Mervis, C. B., Mervis, C. A., Johnson, K. E., & Bertrand, J. (1992). Studying early lexical development: The value of the systematic diary method. In C. Rovee-Collier & L. Lipsitt (Eds.), *Advances in infancy research* (Vol. 7). Norwood, NJ: Ablex.

Molfese, D. L. & Molfese, V. J. (1979). Hemisphere and stimulus differences as reflected in the cortical responses of newborn infants to speech stimuli. *Developmental Psychology*, **15**, 505–511.

Moore, C., Angelopoulos, M., & Bennett, P. (1999). Word learning in the context of referential and salience cues. *Developmental Psychology*, **35**, 60–68.

Morales, M., Mundy, P., & Rojas, J. (1998). Following the direction of gaze and language development in 6-month-olds. *Infant Behavior and Development*, **21**, 373–377.

Murphy, C. M., & Messer, D. J. (1977). Mothers, infants and pointing: A study of a gesture. In H. R. Schaffer (Ed.), *Studies of mother-infant interaction*. London: Academic Press.

Naigles, L. (1990). Children use syntax to learn verb meanings. *Journal of Child Language*, **17**, 357–374.

Namy, L. L. (1998). *What's in a name when it isn't a word? Seventeen month-olds' mapping of non-verbal symbols to object categories*. Manuscript in preparation.

Namy, L. L., & Waxman, S. R. (1998). Words and gestures: Infants' interpretations of different forms of symbolic reference. *Child Development*, **69**, 295–308.

Nelson, K. (1973). Concept, word and sentence: Interrelations in acquisition and development. *Psychological Review*, **81**, 267–295.

Nelson, K. (1988). Constraints on word learning? *Cognitive Development*, **3**, 221–246.

Nelson, K. (1996). *Language in cognitive development*. New York: Cambridge University Press.

Newcombe, N. S. (1998). Defining the "radical middle." *Human Development*, **41**, 210–214.

Newcombe, N. S., & Huttenlocher, J. (in press). *Making space: An interactionist account of development in the spatial domain*. Cambridge, MA: MIT Press.

Oviatt, S. L. (1980). The emerging ability to comprehend language: An experimental approach. *Child Development*, **51**, 97–106.

Piaget, J. (1926). *Language and the thought of the child*. New York: Harcourt, Brace, and World.

Pinker, S. (1994). *The language instinct: How the mind creates language* (1st ed.). New York: William Morrow.

Plunkett, K. (1997). Theories of early language acquisition. *Trends in Cognitive Sciences*, **1**(4), 146–153.

Plunkett, K., & Marchman, V. (1991). U-shaped learning and frequency effects in a multi-layered perceptron: Implications for child language acquisition. *Cognition*, **38**, 43–102.

Plunkett, K., Sinha, C., Moller, M. F., & Strandsby, O. (1992). Symbol grounding or the emergence of symbols? Vocabulary growth in children and a connectionist net. *Connection Science: Journal of Neural Computing, Artificial Intelligence & Cognitive Research*, **4**, 293–312.

Povinelli, D. J., Bering, J. M., & Giambrone, S. (in press). Toward a science of other minds: Escaping the argument by analogy. *Cognitive Science*.

Povinelli, D. J., & Eddy, T. J. (1996). What young chimpanzees know about seeing. *Monographs of the Society for Research in Child Development*, **61**(3, Serial No. 247).

Quine, W. V. O. (1960). *Word and object*. Cambridge, UK: Cambridge University Press.

Rolls, E. T., & Treves, A. (1998). *Neural networks and brain function*. Oxford: Oxford University Press.

Saffran, J. R., Aslin, R. N., & Newport, E. L. (1996). Statistical learning by 8-month-old infants. *Science*, **274**, 1926–1928.

Samuelson, L. K., & Smith, L. B. (1998). Memory and attention make smart word learning: An alternative account of Akhtar, Carpenter, and Tomasello. *Child Development*, **69**, 94–104.

Scaife, M., & Bruner, J. S. (1975). The capacity for joint visual attention in the infant. *Nature*, **253**, 265–266.

Schafer, G., & Plunkett, K. (1998). Rapid word learning by fifteen-month-olds under tightly controlled conditions. *Child Development*, **69**, 309–320.

Schaffer, H. R. (1984). *The child's entry into a social world*. London: Academic Press.

Shafer, V. L., Shucard, D. W., Shucard, J. L., & Gerken, L. A. (1998). An electrophysiological study of infants' sensitivity to the sound patterns of English speech. *Journal of Speech and Hearing Research*, **41**, 874–886.

Shuff, M. M., & Golinkoff, R. M. (1998). *How do young children extend object labels: Perceptual similarity or category membership?* Unpublished manuscript, University of Delaware.

Siegler, R. S. (1996). *Emerging minds*. New York: Oxford University Press.

Smith, L. B. (1995). Self-organizing processes in learning to learn words: Development is not induction. In C. A. Nelson (Ed.), *The Minnesota Symposia on Child Psychology* (Vol. 28). Mahwah, NJ: Erlbaum.

Smith, L. B. (1999). Children's noun learning: How general learning processes make specialized learning mechanisms. In B. MacWhinney (Ed.), *The emergence of language*. Mahwah, NJ: Erlbaum.

Smith, L. B. (in press). Learning how to learn words: An associative crane. In R. M. Golinkoff, K. Hirsh-Pasek, N. Akhtar, L. Bloom, G. Hollich, L. Smith, M. Tomasello, & A. Woodward, *Becoming a word learner: A debate on lexical acquisition*. New York: Oxford Press.

Smith, L. B., Jones, S. S., & Landau, B. (1992). Count nouns, adjectives, and perceptual properties in children's novel word interpretations. *Developmental Psychology*, **28**, 273–286.

Spelke, E. S. (1979). Perceiving bimodally specified events in infancy. *Developmental Psychology*, **15**, 626–636.

Spelke, E. S. (1990). Principles of object perception. *Cognitive Science*, **14**, 29–56.

Spelke, E. S. (1994). Preferential looking and intermodal perception in infancy: Comment on Lewkowicz (1992). *Infant Behavior and Development*, **17**, 285–287.

Stager, C. L., & Werker, J. F. (1997). Infants listen for more phonetic detail in speech perception than in word-learning tasks. *Nature*, **388**, 381–382.

Sternberg, R. J. (1984). *Introduction*. In R. J. Sternberg (Ed.), *Mechanisms of cognitive development*. New York: Freeman.

Templin, M. C. (1957). *Certain language skills in children.* Minneapolis, MN: University of Minnesota Press.

Thelen, E., & Smith, L. B. (1994). *A dynamic systems approach to the development of cognition and action.* Cambridge, MA: The MIT Press.

Tomasello, M. (1995). Joint attention as social cognition. In C. Moore & P. J. Dunham (Eds.), *Joint attention: Its origins and role in development.* Hillsdale, NJ: Lawrence Erlbaum.

Tomasello, M., & Akhtar, N. (1995). Two-year-olds use pragmatic cues to differentiate reference to objects and actions. *Cognitive Development, 10,* 201–224.

Tomasello, M., & Barton, M. (1994). Learning words in non-ostensive context. *Developmental Psychology, 30,* 639–650.

Tomasello, M., & Farrar, J. (1986). Joint attention and early language. *Child Development, 57,* 1454–1463.

Tomasello, M. & Merriman, W. E. (Eds.). (1991). *Beyond names for things: Young children's acquisition of verbs.* Hillsdale, NJ: Erlbaum.

Van Ekeren, G. (1988). *Words for all occasions.* Paramus, NJ: Prentice Hall.

Vygotsky, L. S. (1962). *Thought and language.* Cambridge, MA: MIT Press.

Waxman, S. R., & Kosowski, T. D. (1990). Nouns mark category relations: Toddlers' and preschoolers' word-learning biases. *Child Development, 61,* 1461–1473.

Waxman, S. R., & Markow, D. B. (1995). Words as invitations to form categories: Evidence from 12- to 13-month-old infants. *Cognitive Psychology, 61,* 257–302.

Werker, J. F., Cohen, L. B., Lloyd, V., Stager, C., & Cassosola, M. (1998). Acquisition of word-object associations by 14-month-old infants. *Developmental Psychology, 34,* 1289–1309.

Werker, J. F., & Tees, R. C. (1984). Cross-language speech perception: Evidence for perceptual reorganization during the first year of life. *Infant Behavior and Development, 7,* 49–63.

Werner, H., & Kaplan, E. (1950). Development of word meaning through verbal context: An experimental study. *Journal of Psychology, 29,* 251–257.

Woodward, A. L. (1992). The effect of labeling on children's attention to objects. In E. V. Clark (Ed.), *Proceedings of the 24th Annual Child Language Research Forum.* Chicago: University of Chicago Press.

Woodward, A. L. (1999, April). *Infants' understanding of communicative and non-communicative signals.* Paper presented at the meeting of the Society for Research in Child Development, Albuquerque, NM.

Woodward, A. L., & Hoyne, K. (1999). Infants' learning about words and sounds in relation to objects. *Child Development, 70,* 65–72.

Woodward, A. L., & Markman, E. M. (1998). Early word learning. In D. Kuhn & R. S. Siegler (Eds.), *Handbook of child psychology: Vol. 2. Cognition, perception, and language.* New York: John Wiley & Sons.

Woodward, A. L., Markman, E., & Fitzsimmons, C. M. (1994). Rapid word learning in 13- and 18-month-olds. *Developmental Psychology, 30,* 553–556.

Xu, F. (1998). Distinct labels provide pointers to distinct sortals for 9-month-old infants. In A. Greenhill, M. Hughes, H. Littlefield, & H. Walsh (Eds.), *Proceedings of the 22nd annual Boston University Conference on Language Development* (Vol. 2). Somerville, MA: Cascadilla Press.

Younger, B. A., & Cohen, L. B. (1983). Infant perception of correlations among attributes. *Child Development, 54,* 858–867.

Younger, B. A., & Cohen, L. B. (1986). Developmental changes in infants' perception of correlations among attributes. *Child Development, 57,* 803–815.

Younger, B. A., & Fearing, D. D. (1998). Detecting correlations among form attributes: An object-examining test with infants. *Infant Behavior and Development, 21,* 289–297.

ACKNOWLEDGMENTS

This research was supported by a National Science Foundation grant (#SBR9601306) to the second and third authors and by a National Institute of Child Health and Human Development grant to the second author. We gratefully acknowledge the participation of hundreds of parents and babies in this research. We have also been fortunate to have had many wonderful undergraduate students assist us in our labors and enrich our work. In particular, we thank Michelle McKinney, Kevin Driscoll, Rena Panagos, and Spencer Allen for their contribution. Finally, we express our gratitude to Rachel K. Clifton, who spent countless hours providing us with invaluable editorial guidance on this *Monograph*. For correspondence, please contact George Hollich (ghollich@yahoo.com), Department of Psychology, Ames Hall, Johns Hopkins University, Baltimore, MD 21218; Kathy Hirsh-Pasek (khirshpa@nimbus.ocis.temple.edu), Department of Psychology, Temple University, Philadelphia, PA 19111; or Roberta Golinkoff (Roberta@udel.edu), School of Education, University of Delaware, Newark, DE 19716.

PUSHING THE LIMITS ON THEORIES OF WORD LEARNING

Lois Bloom

The study of children's language traces its history to traditions in psychology and linguistics. From the canon of experimental psychology, we've inherited a strong respect for the "isolated variable" and a concern for avoiding so-called extraneous variables. From linguistics, we've inherited the reverence for language-as-an-object and a disdain for influences from performance. Language is special, its own module, with parts—sounds, words, procedures for sentences—that can be isolated for study. Once we admit *acquisition* into theory and research, however, the object of study can no longer be just the language, by itself. That is because it is a developing *child* who acquires a language, and the process of language acquisition is embedded in the very fabric of the developing child's life. In the real world, variables are not and cannot be isolated. By isolating the units and procedures of the language, or the variables that contribute to its acquisition, the language the child is learning becomes disembodied and decontextualized.

One result of studying only selected variables is that those variables then drive the theories constructed to explain language learning behaviors. The last generation of lexical acquisition research has produced several such theories of word learning that have differed fairly dramatically in vying for the position of truth. Do children learn words because they are somehow endowed with a set of heuristic principles (lexical constraints or biases) that direct them to the right solution for induction of

124

word meaning? Or are children apprenticed to more sophisticated language tutors who set up the world for them in ways that point them to a word's meaning? Or are children good information processors endowed with mechanisms that detect regularities in the input for learning the connections between sounds and meaning? These are the three principal classes of theories that have dominated research in word learning in the last 20 years, and each is well documented by Hollich, Hirsh-Pasek, and Golinkoff in a heroic attempt to bring them together. In calling for a coordinated approach to explain children's word learning, their *Monograph* joins a growing movement toward more integrative theories of word learning (e.g., Bloom, 1993, 1998, 2000; Bloom & Lahey, 1978; Hirsh-Pasek, Golinkoff, & Hollich, 2000; Imai & Haryu, in press; Woodward & Markman, 1998).

The theory and research presented in this *Monograph* are responsive to two fairly straightforward facts. First, infants and children use whatever cues they can for learning about the world and learning the language that is a part of that world (e.g., Bloom, 1973, 1993, 1998; Bloom & Lahey, 1978; Nelson, 1988). None of the narrowly defined theories of the last decade were able to explain the broad range of phenomena children embrace for word learning. Indeed, the major architects of lexical principles theories have, themselves, conceded the importance of the social-pragmatic context, marrying lexical constraints and principles to social-pragmatic cues in the effort to explain how children learn words (Hirsh-Pasek, Golinkoff, & Hollich, 2000; Woodward & Markman, 1998). And, second, the process of word learning changes in the course of development, and theories to explain word learning have to account for developmental change. At the time of emergence, first words are few and far between, fragile, tentative, and imprecise, but 6 months later, on average, word learning is fast, frequent, and robust (e.g., Bloom, 1973, 1993). What happens in the interval between the beginning and the end of the second year of life to explain that difference? By embracing these two facts, in both their theory and research, Hollich et al. make a substantial contribution toward moving the enterprise of understanding children's early word learning forward.

Attempting to build a theoretical consortium, Hollich et al. have pulled together aspects of three disparate and what they describe as "polarized" theories for the more integrative view represented in their "emergentist coalition model." In building a broader base for the lexical principles that form the heart of their model, the authors allow (a) that attentional mechanisms and associative learning have to play a part, particularly at the beginning of word learning, along with (b) the child's social-pragmatic skills, which in their model assume increasing importance toward the end of the 1st year of word learning. Thus, the fundamental appeal in the model comes from the inclusion of multiple, synergistic factors that influence how children words. The model invokes three factors in particular: attentional processes (for making associations), linguistic heuristics (the lexical principles), and social-pragmatic cues (from other persons). They propose that developmental change from 1 to 2 years of age in the process of word learning can be attributed to changes in the relative "weighting" of these factors.

The emergentist coalition model will not suit everyone's theoretical taste. The "hybrid" theory the authors describe merges three very different kinds of theories, with different worldviews. Social-pragmatic theories derive from a contextualist worldview, whereas lexical principles and associative learning come from an inherently mechanistic worldview, and these different worldviews are not considered to be compatible conceptually (Pepper, 1942). The model will, therefore, be viewed by some as too eclectic to be useful, *however much closer it might come to the truth.*

Moreover, attempting to study collaborative influences on behavior and development raises procedural, programmatic, and practical problems that are not easily solved (Bloom, 1993; Bloom & Tinker, 2000). Along with the introduction of the "emergentist coalition model," however, Hollich et al. also introduce an innovative experimental method for studying converging influences on word learning with their *"interactive intermodal preferential looking paradigm."* Its forerunner, Golinkoff and Hirsh-Pasek's earlier intermodal preferential looking paradigm, has already produced a highly influential program of research, and their methodology has been widely adopted by others. Thus, these authors and their colleagues are to be commended, indeed even celebrated, both for advancing the theoretical base for understanding how children begin to learn words, and for continuing to develop and refine research methods for testing their theoretical claims.

By manipulating the variables of object salience, social eye gaze and touch, frequency of exposure, and amount of processing time, among other things, their experiments embraced rather than eliminated the multiple variables that have, in traditional experimental paradigms, been isolated or, worse, eliminated as "extraneous." As a consequence, Hollich et al. come far closer to tapping into how children might make use of multiple cues for learning words in their everyday activities of daily living than have other researchers.

The experiments reported in the *Monograph* are elegant in conceptualization and impressive in the detail with which they probed the limits of word learning by 12-month-old infants, and then compared the relative strength of the word learning cues used by 12-, 18-, and 24-month-olds. I, for one, know of no other experimental studies that have captured the multiple cues that children on the very threshold of language might be using for learning their first words, much less the changes that take place over the course of the 2nd year in the strength of those cues and their coordination. For 12-month-olds, multiple cues must be in alignment and "point" to the same object rather than merely present in the situation, and the dominant cues that capture their attention are perceptual (object salience) rather than social (eye gaze). By 18 and 24 months, perceptual cues become less important, while social cues assume more importance. The authors suggest that this shift between 12 and 24 months, from reliance on perceptual cues to greater use of social cues, explains development in word learning in the 2nd year. Furthermore, younger children "only seem to learn words that correspond to their own perspective" showing, at best, "an immature principle of reference" that depends on the child's own attention to what is perceptually salient. Older children, for whom the principle of reference is now more "mature," can also take another speaker's perspective into account for attaching words to objects.

The description of progress in development from a "child dominated perspective" to a perspective in which the child is able to take another person's intentionality into account is not limited only to word learning by 1-year-olds. For example, the early phrases and simple sentences of 1- to 2-year-old children are "overwhelmingly about what they are just about to do, what they are doing or what they are trying to do, what they want other people to do and, less often, what they see other people doing" (Bloom & Lahey, 1978, p. 134). In studies of the later acquisition of complex sentences that express causality (Bloom & Capatides, 1987; Hood & Bloom, 1979), 2-year-old children's causal expressions were primarily about their own intentions and motivations for acting. Development occurred, however, in progressing from expressing their own intentions in causal statements to taking other persons' intentions into account, first with causally related responses to what someone else said, and then by learning to ask *why* questions. Thus, development from a first-person perspective in expressing the child's own intentionality to a concern for the intentional states of other persons is a more general developmental phenomenon and is not limited to a principle of reference for word learning in the 2nd year.

The model presented in the *Monograph* is a very rich one and the program of research accompanying it no less so. Nevertheless, I have concerns about interpretations surrounding what I see as the dominant issue in the *Monograph*: the nature of *reference* and what develops to influence children's ability to refer. The larger issue of reference in the *Monograph* touches on several other concerns that I will also mention briefly: the persistently myopic focus on *object words* in word learning research, the *phantom child* in the model, and the *missing affect* in theories and research on word learning.

127

Reference

The major emphasis in the book is on the authors' "principle of reference," which they describe as foundational, in the "first tier" of word learning principles they see as necessary to get word learning started. However, the "development of reference is a mystery, a mystery that forms the cornerstone of this *Monograph*." Consistent with the way in which the notion of "reference" is ordinarily conceived, the children in these studies only had experiences mapping words to available objects, under varying conditions of presentation. Although the authors allow in passing that reference has an intervening cognitive dimension, their accounts of referring typically describe observable events, the mapping between word and object in the world.

Words do not map directly to objects and events in the external world, however, and such accounts of reference bypass the unobservable, internal dimension of language. It is the mental elements set up and represented in intentional states that are directed at objects, events, and relations and that do the referring, not words. "Language forms do not *refer* to such elements. If there is to be reference, it will go from the elements in mental spaces [intentional states] to the objects referred to" (Fauconnier, 1985, p. 2). Words a child says name such *mental* elements in acts of expression, and words the child hears set up such mental elements in intentional states for acts of interpretation. Thus, while learning words is a linguistic activity, referring is a mental activity. Children learn words that embody intentional states—that express and also articulate the elements, roles, and relations that refer to what they understand about objects, events, and relations in the world. Understanding how words relate to things requires understanding the *activity* by which words and things are related, and that activity of referring is mental, not linguistic (Taylor, 1985).

The authors assume that "by the time infants are learning their first words, the principle of reference is already available," albeit in an "immature" form. "Even 12-month-olds, at some level, assume that words refer" although it is not until the 2nd year that a mature principle of reference is available for word learning. According to Hollich et al., the immature principle at the beginning of word learning depends only on associative connections. When the mature principle of reference emerges by the end of the 2nd year, words have symbolic status and can "stand for" what is referred to. The immature principle is an associative one; the mature principle is a symbolic one—reminiscent of Piaget's (1954) description of development in this same period of time. For Piaget, the intervening developments were explicitly cognitive. The lexical principle of reference, however, seems to have a life of its own. Where then does the principle of reference come from?

Theories based on lexical principles, in general, originated in the domain-specific constraints theories that have been hypothesized to narrow the range of acceptable inputs for development in a variety of cognitive domains, such as number (e.g., Gelman & Williams, 1998). The original assumption was that such a priori constraints were given and necessarily innate, so that learning might be guided from the beginning. More recent claims for word learning constraints, in particular, have been decidedly muted with respect to innateness, with a growing consensus that lexical principles evolve with development at the same time that they guide word learning. Nonetheless, Hollich et al. describe the principle of reference as an "initial bias," necessarily present from the beginning if word learning is to ever get started, but the principle also undergoes developmental change. "As a result of word learning experience, children form ever more refined hypotheses about the way words work," until the mature principle of reference is available at about age 2 or some time after the vocabulary spurt, evidently *as a consequence of word learning*.

The presumption that lexical principles develop over time is a notable feature of the theoretical position in the *Monograph*. But if words develop from a "goes together" (associative) relationship at the beginning of the period to a "stands for" (symbolic) relationship at the end of the period, then what contribution comes from the external lexical principle over and above the cognitive developments that are implicit in the process? And if, indeed, a principle of reference is itself developing at the same time that words are being acquired, can the principle also be the "heuristic" the child uses to test alternative hypotheses about what a word might mean, and thereby explain developmental change? Or, more likely, is the principle a convenient and accurate *description*, after the fact, of the developmental changes that take place in the process of word learning? If lexical principles evolve as children acquire a vocabulary, they might more appropriately *describe* what it is about the language that children are learning—what children are learning about words and how they work— than *explain* how that learning takes place (Bloom, 1993; 1998; Bloom, Tinker, & Margulis, 1994; Nelson, 1988).

The authors keep circling back to their wonderment over how word learning could ever get off the ground without a principle of reference to begin with: "It is hard to imagine word learning without the central principle of reference"; echoing MacNamara (1982), "It is hard to imagine how children would acquire a principle of reference if they did not start out with one"; and, finally, "Input would be irrelevant if reference was not present in some form in the first place." However much they may wonder, it seems to me that they have, in fact, done it! They have, in fact, shown how reference develops and what sorts of input children make

129

use of in the process of that development. They have managed to tease apart some of the cues available in word learning situations and demonstrated the relative weights those cues have at different times in the early word learning period. Having read the *Monograph*, I, for one, am now satisfied that it really isn't such a "mystery" at all. By the time infants are able to make their first word-meaning associations toward the end of the 1st year, they have already had considerable experience with linguistic input and demonstrated fairly impressive skills in processing that input (e.g., Jusczyk et al., 1992). They have also already had a year of learning about the world so that they can begin to put their emerging conceptual knowledge together with their increasingly sophisticated perception of linguistic signals to form connections between sound and meaning.

In sum, the principle of reference develops along a continuum, from describing a "goes-with" relationship in an association to a decontextualized "stands-for" relationship—from an immature principle whereby a label is attached to whatever is "interesting" based on *perceptual* cues, to a mature principle when the child is apprenticed to adults who lead or direct the child's attention to a word's meaning. The continuum is from perceptually based, associationist learning to social learning. But is it the *principle* itself that develops? Or is it *the child's ability to refer* that develops? And if it is the child's ability to refer that develops, then why is it necessary to call it a "principle"?

Which brings us back to the question, where does the principle of reference come from? There is an alternative to the assumption in the *Monograph* that "initial biases [such as the albeit immature principle of reference] must exist." I suspect that the changes in word learning that take place in the 2nd year are epiphenomenal—a by-product of developments in perception, cognition, and social sensitivity, rather than attributable to development of the specifically lexical principle of reference offered to explain it. In fact, the authors do allow that along with their other first-tier principles, reference "may be rooted in cognitive-perceptual development" rather than being specifically linguistic at the beginning of word learning. If that is so, then why must a principle of reference exist, a priori, to guide word learning?

The development required for the mental activity of referring includes two things, at least. First is development in the *symbolic capacity* for making possible the representations in mind—the elements, roles, and relationships in intentional states—that refer to what a child understands of objects and events in the world. Arguably, this was the hallmark of Piaget's (1954) theory for development of the processes of active thought that determine a child's actions. The heart of this development, in his theory, takes place in the 2nd year of life, coinciding with the emergence of words and development of the early lexicon. Second is the formation of *concepts* and conceptual structure in the knowledge base that inform what the child's contents of mind, intentional states, are about. Surely word learning in the 2nd year depends as much on children's emerging concepts as on their ability to form associations and social-pragmatic skills (e.g., Bates, 1979; Bloom, 1973, 1993; Bloom & Lahey, 1978; Clark, 1973, 1974; Nelson, 1974). This basic fact, however, seems to have been lost in recent word learning research.

Thus, Hollich et al. are correct in assuming that the activity of referring is "rooted in" developments in cognition and perception. Moreover, referring is a mental activity, not linguistic, and is the ordinary thinking that goes into word learning. The same mental activity, therefore, has to go into learning any kind of word, not just the sort of object names that have been the focus of research on lexical principles.

Object Words, Again

Reference, as it is ordinarily conceived, cannot work for words like "more" or "up" or "gone," which are among children's earliest and most frequent words, because such words do not name objects that are "out there" in the world. But 1-year-old children have no difficulty constructing intentional state representations that refer to their understanding of the relationships named by these words, and they learn many such words from the start of word learning (e.g., Bates et al., 1994; Bloom, 1973; Bloom et al., 1994; Gopnik, 1982, 1988; Lieven, Pine, & Barnes, 1992; McCune-Nicolich, 1981; Nelson, 1973; Nelson, Hampson, & Shaw, 1993; Pine, 1992a, 1992b). Theories based on lexical constraints, principles, or biases have by and large, however, ignored the whole class of words that do not have object-boundedness.

Although Hollich et al. mention that other kinds of words, particularly verbs, also might be learned through lexical principles, the theory and the research they've presented are about how children learn object names. Even if verbs and other words that are not object names represent less than half, or a quarter, or only a tenth of a child's first 50 words, object specific principles cannot explain early word learning unless the principles themselves are tinkered with by building in ad hoc procedures for "overriding" them (Markman, 1989). Moreover, the claim that "to date, there has been relatively little research on how children learn their first action words" is true only for experimental research into constraints and principles. A whole literature exists on verb learning in the context of how children learn procedures for sentences (see Bloom, 1991, for some examples and citations of other studies).

131

The Phantom Child in the Model

It is hard for me to see what contribution the child learner in the emergentist coalition model is making to the process of word learning except in the relatively passive roles as a *perceiver* of physical cues, the *receiver* of social cues, and somehow the *possessor* of constraints, biases, or heuristic principles that filter the available information for the child. Missing is the *authority of the child* in the acquisition process. What a child has in mind—the child's intentional state at any particular moment of time—determines the child's actions and interactions in the world and, hence, the child's development (Bloom, 1993). Where is there a place for the child's active, on-line thinking that goes on in the moments of word learning—the ordinary thinking (reflecting, considering) in the "here and now" of the child's intentionality? And where in the model does the child access the concepts and conceptual structure in the knowledge base on which learning the meanings of words depends?

The Missing Affect in the Model

The relative salience of an object does not itself determine what is "interesting" for learning, if it ignores the *value* of the child's affective response to the object, or the child's affective investment in the task, or affective investment in the individuals in the situation. In the Hollich et al. model, learning from perception depends only on "salience," and objects in an experiment can be made more or less salient. But it is not just the perception of salience that leads to learning a word's meaning. If a child wants a cookie and sees the cookie next to a big, green dog, the child will focus on the less conspicuous cookie, when it is *relevant* to what the child has in mind, that is, when the child wants the cookie. Of course, the child's attention may be deliberately called to the salience of the dog, and the child may be easily distracted (depending on when and how that green dog appears). But children learn the words for many things that are not particularly salient in the perceptible context. Relevance, not salience, determines whether words are worth learning, and the child's affective appraisals are a major contributor to relevance (Bloom, 1993).

Concluding Thoughts

When one looks back on the history of the study of word learning in the last quarter century, two very different empirical paradigms have each made their contributions. This last generation of experimental work inspired by principles and constraints theory clearly moved the enterprise of understanding word learning forward, and the authors of this *Monograph* have been leaders in that movement. At the same time, the results of observational studies in the tradition that began with the 19th-century diarists and continue today have made no less a contribution and just as clearly provided insights into children's word learning—insights that are often echoed in the experimental studies. Arguably, criticisms of constraints and principles theories from the observational perspective played a part in determining how theory and research based on lexical principles evolved in the last decade, perhaps even culminating in the present *Monograph*. Nevertheless, observational studies are not usually credited for the influence they obviously have had on raising awareness of issues, particularly the importance of the social-pragmatic context and more general cognition, that have to be taken seriously in the enterprise of studying how children learn words.

The questions I've raised here by no means diminish the considerable accomplishments represented in this *Monograph*. Hollich et al. have taken a giant step toward understanding the converging inputs that contribute to word learning. I am only calling for more than they have already done, which may not be entirely fair. But future generations of word learning theories will have to come to terms with the fact that children in the typical, everyday word learning scenario are more than perceivers, receivers, or possessors of external supports. Instead, the word learning child is a child with feelings and thoughts about other persons, a child engaged in dynamic real-life events, a child learning to think about a world of changing physical and psychological relationships—in short, a child poised to act, to influence, to gain control, a child reaching out to embrace the learning of language for the power of expression it provides.

REFERENCES

Bates, E. (1979). *The emergence of symbols: Communication and cognition in infancy.* New York: Academic Press.

Bates, E., Marchman, V., Thal, D., Fenson, L., Dale, P., Reznick, S., Reilly, J., & Hartung, J. (1994). Developmental and stylistic variation in the composition of early vocabulary. *Journal of Child Language,* **21**, 85–123.

Bloom, L. (1973). *One word at a time: The use of single-word utterances before syntax.* The Hague: Mouton.

Bloom, L. (1991). *Language development from two to three.* Cambridge: Cambridge University Press.

Bloom, L. (1993). *The transition from infancy to language: Acquiring the power of expression.* Cambridge: Cambridge University Press.

Bloom, L. (1998). Language acquisition in its developmental context. In W. Damon (Series Ed.) & D. Kuhn & R. Siegler (Vol. Eds.), *Handbook of child psychology: Vol. II. Cognition, perception, and language.* New York: Wiley.

Bloom, L. (2000). The intentionality model of language development: How to learn a word, any word. In R. Golinkoff, K. Hirsh-Pasek, N. Akhtar, L. Bloom, G. Hollich, L. Smith, M. Tomasello, & A. Woodward, *Becoming a word learner: A debate on lexical acquisition.* New York: Oxford University Press.

Bloom, L., & Capatides, J. (1987). Sources of meaning in complex syntax: The sample case of causality. *Journal of Experimental Child Psychology,* **43**, 112–128.

Bloom, L., & Lahey, M. (1978). *Language development and language disorders.* New York: Wiley.

Bloom, L., & Tinker, E. (2000). *The coordination of engagement and effort for acquiring a language.* Unpublished manuscript.

Bloom, L., Tinker, E., & Margulis, C. (1994). The words children learn: Evidence against a noun bias in children's vocabularies. *Cognitive Development,* **8**, 431–450.

Clark, E. (1973). Non-linguistic strategies and the acquisition of word meanings. *Cognition,* **2**, 161–182.

Clark, E. (1974). Some aspects of the conceptual basis for first language acquisition. In R. Schiefelbusch & L. Lloyd (Eds.), *Language perspectives—Acquisition, retardation, and intervention.* Baltimore, MD: University Park Press.

Fauconnier, G. (1985). *Mental spaces: Aspects of meaning construction in natural language.* Cambridge, MA: MIT Press.

Gelman, R., & Williams, E. (1998). Enabling constraints for cognitive development and learning: Domain specificity and epigenesis. In W. Damon (Series Ed.) & D. Kuhn & R. Siegler (Vol. Eds.), *Handbook of child psychology: Vol. II. Cognition, perception, and language.* New York: Wiley.

Gopnik, A. (1982). Words and plans: Early language and the development of intelligent action. *Journal of Child Language*, **9**, 303–318.

Gopnik, A. (1988). Three types of early word: The emergence of social words, names and cognitive-relational words in the one-word stage and their relation to cognitive development. *First Language*, **8**, 49–70.

Hirsh-Pasek, K., Golinkoff, R., & Hollich, G. (2000). An emergentist coalition model for word learning: Mapping words to objects is a product of the interaction of multiple cues. In R. Golinkoff, K. Hirsh-Pasek, N. Akhtar, L. Bloom, G. Hollich, L. Smith, M. Tomasello, & A. Woodward, *Becoming a word learner: A debate on lexical acquisition.* New York: Oxford University Press.

Imai, M., & Haryu, E. (in press). How do Japanese children learn proper nouns and common nouns without clues from syntax? *Child Development.*

Hood, L., & Bloom, L. (1979). What, when, and how about why: A longitudinal study of early expressions of causality. *Monographs of the Society for Research in Child Development*, **44**(6, Serial No. 181).

Jusczyk, P., Hirsh-Pasek, K., Kemler Nelson, D., Kennedy, L., Woodward, A., & Piwoz, J. (1992). Perception of acoustic correlates of major phrasal boundaries by young infants. *Cognitive Psychology*, **24**, 252–293.

Lieven, E., Pine, J., & Barnes, H. (1992). Individual differences in early vocabulary development: Redefining the referential-expressive distinction. *Journal of Child Language*, **19**, 287–310.

MacNamara, J. (1982). *Names for things.* Cambridge, MA: The MIT Press.

Markman, E. (1989). *Categorization and naming in children.* Cambridge, MA: MIT Press.

McCune-Nicolich, L. (1981). The cognitive basis of relational words in the single word period. *Journal of Child Language*, **8**, 15–34.

Nelson, K. (1973). Structure and strategy in learning to talk. *Monographs of the Society for Research in Child Development*, **38**(1–2, Serial No. 149).

Nelson, K. (1974). Concept, word and sentence: Interrelations in acquisition and development. *Psychological Review*, **81**, 267–285.

Nelson, K. (1988). Constraints on word learning. *Cognitive Development*, **3**, 221–246.

Nelson, K., Hampson, J., & Shaw, L. (1993). Nouns in early lexicons: Evidence, explanations, and implications. *Journal of Child Language*, **20**, 61–84.

Pepper, S. (1942). *World hypotheses: A study in evidence.* Berkeley and Los Angeles: University of California Press.

Piaget, J. (1954). *The construction of reality in the child.* New York: Basic Books. (Original work published 1937)

Pine, J. (1992a). How referential are "referential" children? Relationships between maternal-report and observational measures of vocabulary composition and usage. *Journal of Child Language*, **19**, 75–86.

Pine, J. (1992b). The functional basis of referentiality: Evidence from children's spontaneous speech. *First Language*, **12**, 39–55.

Taylor, C. (1985). *Philosophical papers: Vol. 1. Human agency and language.* Cambridge: Cambridge University Press.

Woodward, A., & Markman, E. (1998). Early word learning. In W. Damon (Series Ed.) & D. Kuhn & R. Siegler (Eds.), *Handbook of child psychology: Vol. II. Cognition, perception, and language.* New York: John Wiley & Sons.

Rebecca J. Brand (B.A., 1996, Vassar College) coordinated the Infant Language Project at the University of Delaware and is a graduate student at the University of Oregon. Her research focuses on the social and cognitive aspects of early language development.

Ellie Brown (B.A., 2000, Haverford College) was a research assistant at the Infant Language Project at the University of Delaware and is presently a student at Haverford College. She plans to continue her training in clinical psychology.

He Len Chung (B.A., 1994, Washington College) coordinated the Infant Language Project at the University of Delaware and is presently a graduate student in clinical psychology at Temple University who is interested in adolescence and cross-cultural psychology.

Roberta Michnick Golinkoff (Ph.D., 1973, Cornell University) is H. Rodney Sharp Professor of Education, Psychology, and Linguistics at the University of Delaware. Much of her work focuses on early language acquisition in both the lexical and syntactic domain. She has been the recipient of a James McKeen Cattell Sabbatical Award and a John Simon Guggenheim Memorial Fellowship. Publications include: Golinkoff, R., & Hirsh-Pasek, K. (1999). *How Babies Talk.* New York, Dutton/Penguin; Golinkoff, R. M., Hirsh-Pasek, K., Akhtar, N., Bloom, L., Hollich, G., Smith, L., Tomasello, M., & Woodward, A. (in press). *Becoming a Word Learner: A Debate on Lexical Acquisition.* New York: Oxford Press; and three edited books. She has been on the editorial boards of *Child Development, Monographs of the Society for Research in Child Development, The Journal of Educational Psychology,* and *Developmental Psychology.*

Elizabeth Hennon (B.A., 1996, Pennsylvania State University) is a graduate student at Temple University. Her research focuses on speech pathology and language development.

Kathy Hirsh-Pasek (Ph.D., 1981, University of Pennsylvania) is a professor of psychology at Temple University. Her primary research focuses on early language development in children zero-to-three emphasizing how infants process the input in ways that assist them in learning words and grammar. She also focuses on issues within cognitive development that bridge the gap between science and policy. As such, she conducted research on the "hurried child," and is one of the investigators in the NICHD Study of Early Child Care. Publications include: Hirsh-Pasek, K., & Golinkoff, R. (1996) *The Origins of Grammar: Evidence From Early Language Comprehension.* Cambridge, MIT Press; and Rescorla, L., Hyson, M., & Hirsh-Pasek, K. (1991) "Academic Instruction in Early Childhood: Challenge or Pressure?" In W. Damon (Gen. Ed.), *New directions in developmental psychology, 53,* New York: Jossey-Bass. Dr. Hirsh-Pasek is on the editorial board of *Child Development* and *Infancy.*

George Hollich (Ph.D., 1999, Temple University) is a postdoctoral fellow at Johns Hopkins University. His current research interests include computational modeling of language learning, testing of infant language comprehension and speech perception, and the development of domain-specific skills from domain-general mechanisms.

Camille Rocroi (B.A., 1998, Temple University) coordinated the Temple University Infant Laboratories and is currently a graduate student at Johns Hopkins University. Her research interests include language development, effectiveness of early childhood interventions, and language skills in autism.

Lois Bloom (Ph.D., 1968, Columbia University) is Edward Lee Thorndike Professor Emeritus, Teachers College, Columbia University.

STATEMENT OF EDITORIAL POLICY

The *Monographs* series is intended as an outlet for major reports of developmental research that generate authoritative new findings and use these to foster a fresh and/or better integrated perspective on some conceptually significant issue or controversy. Submissions from programmatic research projects are particularly welcome; these may consist of individually or group-authored reports of findings from some single large-scale investigation or of a sequence of experiments centering on some particular question. Multiauthored sets of independent studies that center on the same underlying question can also be appropriate; a critical requirement in such instances is that the various authors address common issues and that the contribution arising from the set as a whole be both unique and substantial. In essence, irrespective of how it may be framed, any work that contributes significant data and/or extends developmental thinking will be taken under editorial consideration.

Submissions should contain a minimum of 80 manuscript pages (including tables and references); the upper limit of 150–175 pages is much more flexible (please submit four copies; a copy of every submission and associated correspondence is deposited eventually in the archives of the SRCD). Neither membership in the Society for Research in Child Development nor affiliation with the academic discipline of psychology is relevant; the significance of the work in extending developmental theory and in contributing new empirical information is by far the most crucial consideration. Because the aim of the series is not only to advance knowledge on specialized topics but also to enhance cross-fertilization among disciplines or subfields, it is important that the links between the specific issues under study and larger questions relating to developmental processes emerge as clearly to the general reader as to specialists on the given topic.

Potential authors who may be unsure whether the manuscript they are planning would make an appropriate submission are invited to draft an outline of what they propose and send it to the Editor for assessment. This mechanism, as well as a more detailed description of all editorial policies, evaluation processes, and format requirements, is given in the "Guidelines for the Preparation of *Monographs* Submissions," which can be obtained by contacting the Editor Designate, Willis Overton, Department of Psychology, 567 Weiss Hall, Temple University, Philadelphia, PA 19122 (e-mail: overton@vm.temple.edu).